Easy WordPerfect® 6
for Windows™, 2nd Edition

Trudi Reisner

Easy WordPerfect 6 for Windows, 2nd Edition

Copyright© 1994 by Que® Corporation.

Library of Congress Catalog No.: 94-65889

ISBN: 1-56529-809-8

97 96 95   4 3

Interpretation of the printing code: the rightmost double-digit number is the year of the book's printing; the rightmost single-digit number, the number of the book's printing. For example, a printing code of 94-1 shows that the first printing of the book occurred in 1994.

Publisher: David P. Ewing

Associate Publisher: Michael Miller

Publishing Director: Don Roche, Jr.

Managing Editor: Michael Cunningham

Marketing Manager: Ray Robinson

Credits

Publishing Manager
Charles O. Stewart III

Acquisitions Editor
Thomas F. Godfrey III

Product Directors
Kathie-Jo Arnoff
Lisa D. Wagner

Production Editor
Thomas F. Hayes

Copy Editors
Jeanne Lemen
Susan Ross Moore

Technical Editor
Phil Sabotin

Book Designer
Amy Peppler-Adams

Cover Designer
Jay Corpus

Production Team
Stephen Adams
Claudia Bell
Anne Dickerson
Karen Dodson
Teresa Forrester
Joelynn Gifford
Bob LaRoche
Jay Lesandrini
Elizabeth Lewis
Andrea Marcum
Tim Montgomery
Wendy Ott
Nanci Sears Perry
Linda Quigley
Dennis Sheehan
Amy Steed
Michael Thomas
Sue VandeWalle
Mary Beth Wakefield

Indexer
Michael Hughes

Composed in *Stone Serif* and *MCPDigital* by Que Corporation.

Dedication

To Terri Digiro, with special thanks for her encouragement and support.

About the Author

Trudi Reisner is a computer consultant specializing in training users of IBM PCs, PC compatibles, and Apple Macintoshes in the use of applications software. She is the owner of Computer Training Solutions, a Boston, Mass., company that offers training, technical writing, curriculum development, and consulting services in software programs.

Trudi has written numerous books on WordPerfect and other software including Que's *Allways Quick Reference, Ami Pro 3 Quick Reference, Easy 1-2-3 Release 4 for Windows, Easy Excel 5 for Windows, Easy Word Version 6 for Windows, Excel VisiRef, Harvard Graphics 3 Quick Reference, Quattro Pro 4 Quick Reference,* and *Word for Windows 2 Quick Reference.* She also is a contributing author to *Using Ami Pro 3 for Windows, Special Edition.*

Acknowledgments

I owe thanks to many who helped complete this book. Foremost is Product Director Lisa Wagner for her competent skills, who edited the manuscript and gave suggestions and support throughout the life of this project; and Production Editor Tom Hayes, who managed the copy editing process for this project. Also, thanks to Chuck Stewart for his guidance in the structure and design of this book.

Special recognition must go to Acquisitions Editor Tom Godfrey for his outstanding management skills, who suggested the project, and gave support and encouragement throughout the project.

Also, many thanks to the technical editors, whose timely proofing helped maintain the accuracy of the text from cover to cover. Special thanks to the production staff who turned the final draft on disk into this printed copy in record time—a monumental task.

Finally, thanks to WordPerfect Corporation, who developed and produced a fine word processing program.

Trademark Acknowledgments

All terms mentioned in this book that are known to be trademarks or service marks have been appropriately capitalized. Que cannot attest to the accuracy of this information. Use of a term in this book should not be regarded as affecting the validity of any trademark or service mark. Trademarks indicated below were derived from various sources.

WordPerfect is a registered trademark and Button Bar is a trademark of WordPerfect Corporation.

Contents at a Glance

Table of Contents

Part VI: More Formatting   134

Part VII: Enhancing Your Document   154

Part VIII: Viewing and Printing the Document   182

Introduction

What You Can Do with WordPerfect

WordPerfect for Windows is one of the world's most popular word processing software programs. You could create documents on a typewriter, but WordPerfect makes writing, editing, and printing them easier.

Specifically, you can use WordPerfect to perform these functions:

- *Correct errors.* With a typewriter, after you press a key, that letter is committed to paper. To correct a mistake, you have to use correctors such as liquid paper, or retype the document. With WordPerfect, you see the text on-screen. You can easily correct any typographical errors *before* you print the document.

- *Move around quickly.* With the document on-screen, you can move from one sentence, paragraph, or page to another. You can move quickly from the top of the document to the bottom and vice versa.

- *Make editing changes.* You can insert text into any location in your document. You also can delete any amount of text quickly—a character, a word, a sentence, a paragraph, or a block of text.

- *Rearrange your text.* When you sit down to write, you don't always write in order from the introduction to the summary. Ideas may occur to you in a different order. As you're writing the summary, for example, you might think of an idea that belongs in the introduction. With WordPerfect, you can write when you think of it, and then easily move and copy the text from one location to another.

- *Restore deleted text.* When you accidentally delete text that you want to keep, you don't have to retype it. Instead, you can just restore the text to its original state. Also, WordPerfect's Undo feature enables you to undo errors.

- *Check spelling.* Before you print, you can run a spell check to search for misspellings and double words. If you are a poor typist, this feature enables you to concentrate on your writing and leave spelling errors for WordPerfect to catch.

- *Search for text.* You can search your document for a particular word or phrase. For example, you can move quickly to the section of your document that discusses expenditures by searching for the word *expenditures.*

- *Search and replace text.* You can make text replacements throughout the document quickly and easily. For example, you can change all occurrences of the name *Smith* to *Smythe*.

- *Make formatting changes.* WordPerfect enables you to easily change margins, tabs, and other formatting options. You can experiment with the settings until the document appears the way you want it. Then you print it.

- *Change how text is printed.* You can boldface, italicize, and underline text. WordPerfect also lets you shade paragraphs and add borders. You also can use a different typeface, depending on your printer.

- *Preview your document.* You can preview your document to see how it looks when you print. If you want to make changes before you print, you can do this in any view of your document.

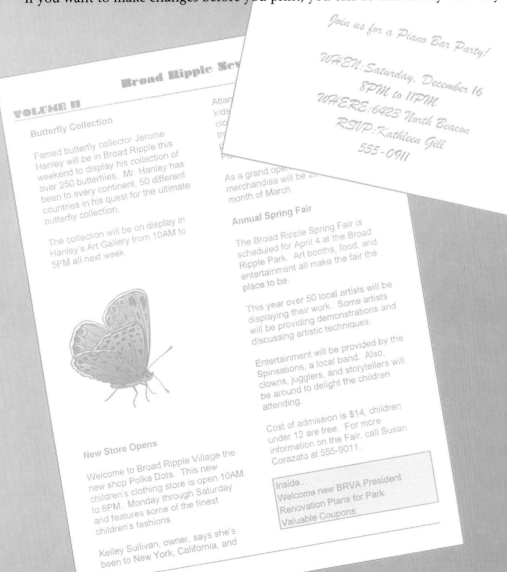

Task Sections

The Task sections include numbered steps that tell you how to accomplish certain tasks, such as saving a document, or indenting a paragraph. The numbered steps walk you through a specific example so that you learn the task by actually doing it.

Big Screen

At the beginning of each task is a large screen shot that shows how the computer screen looks after you complete the procedure described in that task. Sometimes the screen shot shows a feature discussed in that task, such as the Go To dialog box.

TASK 7

Adding Text

"Why would I do this?"

Normally, WordPerfect is in Insert mode. In Insert mode, you type text at the insertion point and the existing text moves forward to make room for the new text. In WordPerfect for Windows, you may find that you need to change a document by adding or replacing text after the document is complete.

In the following task, first hide the Ruler Bar; then display the Power Bar. That way, you can use the Power Bar tools at any time during the exercises. Then, enter text for the first chapter of a manuscript, and finally, insert additional text.

30

Step-by-Step Screens

Each task includes a screen shot for each step
of a procedure.

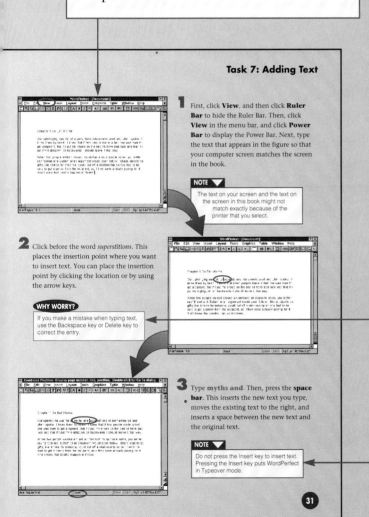

Task 7: Adding Text

1 First, click **View**, and then click **Ruler Bar** to hide the Ruler Bar. Then, click **View** in the menu bar, and click **Power Bar** to display the Power Bar. Next, type the text that appears in the figure so that your computer screen matches the screen in the book.

NOTE ▼

The text on your screen and the text on the screen in this book might not match exactly because of the printer that you select.

2 Click before the word *superstitions*. This places the insertion point where you want to insert text. You can place the insertion point by clicking the location or by using the arrow keys.

WHY WORRY?

If you make a mistake when typing text, use the Backspace key or Delete key to correct the entry.

3 Type **myths and**. Then, press the **space bar**. This inserts the new text you type, moves the existing text to the right, and inserts a space between the new text and the original text.

NOTE ▼

Do not press the Insert key to insert text. Pressing the Insert key puts WordPerfect in Typeover mode.

31

Why Worry? Notes

You may find that you performed a task—such as underlining text—that you really didn't want to do. The Why Worry? notes tell you how to undo certain procedures or get out of a situation, such as reversing a procedure or getting out of a mode.

Other Notes

Many tasks include other short notes that tell you a little more about certain procedures. These notes define terms, explain other options, refer you to other sections when applicable, and so on.

PART I
Learning the Basics

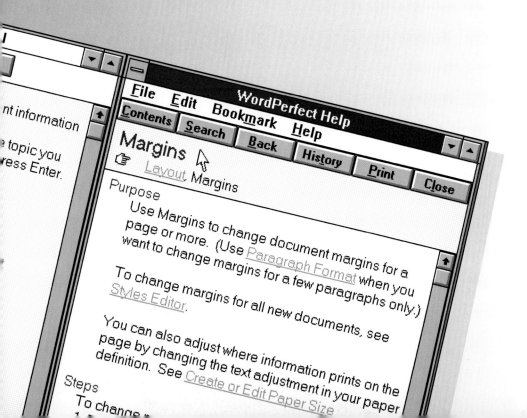

Part I of this book introduces you to WordPerfect basics. You need to know some fundamental things about WordPerfect before you start creating your own documents.

In this part, you learn how to start and exit WordPerfect. You should ensure that WordPerfect is installed on your hard disk so that it appears in your Windows Program Manager as a program icon. For installation instructions, refer to your WordPerfect for Windows documentation. You can start and exit WordPerfect as you would any Windows application.

When you start the program, WordPerfect displays a blank document—much like a blank piece of paper. The document is a file in which you store your data.

The menu bar is just below the title bar at the top of the screen. This bar displays the main menu names. In Part I you learn how to select a menu command. If you prefer to keep your hands on the keyboard, learn the shortcut keys that appear in the menus next to the command names. This book notes some shortcut keys in the exercises.

When you select a menu command followed by an ellipsis (...), WordPerfect displays a dialog box. The dialog box is an on-screen box that asks you for additional information. When a menu command is followed by an arrow, selecting that menu command displays another menu (called a *cascading menu*). To select a menu command from the second menu, click the menu command you want.

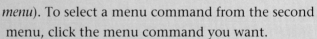

The *Power Bar* that appears below the menu bar provides quick access to commands that you use frequently. If you don't use the Power Bar, you might want to hide it. In this part, you learn how to hide the Power Bar.

WordPerfect ships with several *Button Bars* that provide quick access to the most common WordPerfect commands. The Button Bars contain tools you use for formatting a document, drawing graphics in the document, merging files, and other WordPerfect operations. See your WordPerfect documentation for complete information on Button Bars. This part shows you how to display the Button Bar.

The *Ruler Bar* enables you to make formatting changes quickly. You can change tabs, set margins, and much more. See your WordPerfect documentation for complete information on the Ruler Bar. In this part, you learn how to display the Ruler Bar.

The *insertion point* is a flashing vertical bar that appears in the document window. Text that you type appears at the position of the insertion point.

This part also discusses some of the ways you can get help in WordPerfect. To get instant on-line help, look at How Do I, Macros, Coach, and Tutorial.

The tasks that follow in this part teach essential skills you need to perform many of WordPerfect's operations.

TASK 1

Starting and Exiting WordPerfect for Windows

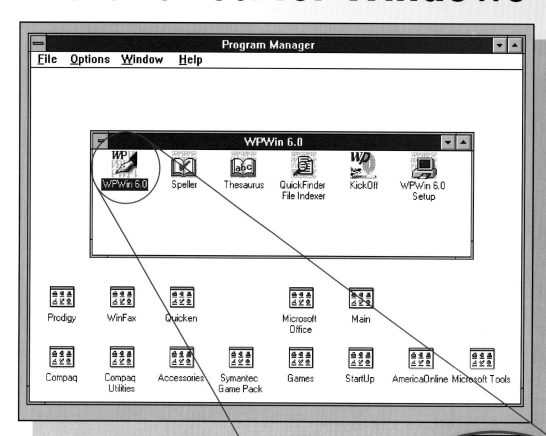

"Why would I do this?"

Starting WordPerfect is simple to do—once you've done it, it's as easy as starting the engine in your car! When you no longer want to work in WordPerfect, you can exit WordPerfect and return to the Windows Program Manager.

This task assumes you have turned on your computer and started Microsoft Windows. Jump right in and start WordPerfect. Later, we will exit WordPerfect.

Task 1: Starting and Exiting WordPerfect for Windows

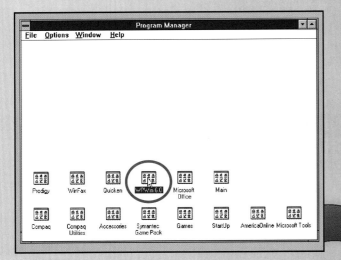

1 Double-click the group icon for **WPWin 6.0**. The group icon is the icon for the program group where you stored WordPerfect when you installed the program. This book assumes that you stored the program in a program group called WPWin 6.0. To double-click the group icon, move the mouse pointer to the group icon and click the left mouse button twice in rapid succession.

2 Double-click the program icon for **WPWin 6.0**, or click the WPWin 6.0 icon and press Enter. This starts the WordPerfect program.

NOTE ▼

If the program group is open, you only need to click the existing program group to make it active, not double-click the group icon. You also can open the WPWin 6.0 group by clicking Window in the menu bar, and then clicking WPWin 6.0.

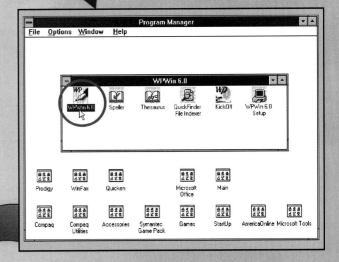

3 A blank document appears in a window on-screen. (Each time you start the program, the start-up screen with your name and the license agreement appears before the blank document.)

NOTE ▼

To prevent data loss, be sure that you save any changed documents and exit WordPerfect before turning off the computer.

Task 1: Starting and Exiting WordPerfect for Windows

4 Click **File** in the menu bar. This step opens the File menu. You see a list of File commands. Click **Exit**. This selects the **Exit** command.

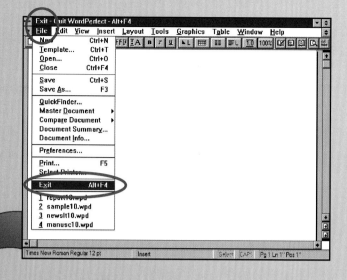

NOTE ▼

To quickly exit WordPerfect, double-click the Control menu box. This box is the small bar to the left of the WordPerfect window's title bar.

5 You return to the Windows Program Manager.

WHY WORRY?

When you're using the mouse to execute a command, make sure you double-click the left mouse button. If nothing happens, or if the icon slides around, check the location of the mouse pointer and try double-clicking again.

Selecting a Menu Command

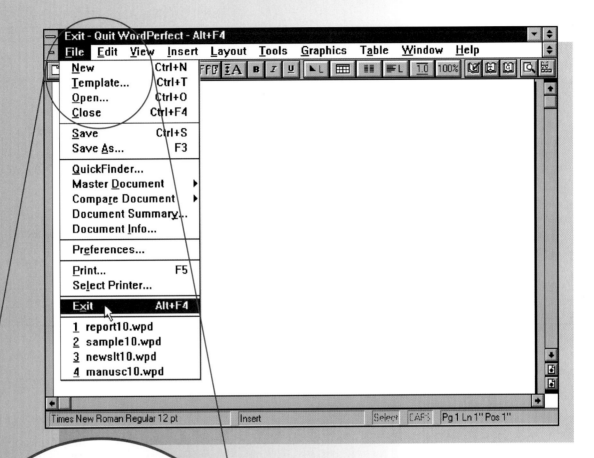

"Why would I do this?"

WordPerfect's menu bar is located directly below the application window's title bar. This line contains pull-down menus that list WordPerfect commands. You need these commands for the currently selected cell(s) or an object such as a chart. You might want to use a command to edit or format text.

Let's examine how to select a menu command.

Task 2: Selecting a Menu Command

1 Start WordPerfect as you did in Task 1. A blank document appears on-screen.

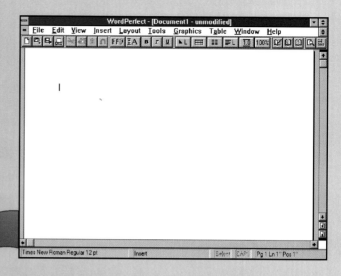

2 Point to **File** in the menu bar and click the left mouse button. This step opens the menu. In this case, you are opening the File menu. You see a list of File commands.

3 Point to **New** and click the left mouse button. This selects the command. In this case, you are selecting the New command. You see a blank document in the window on-screen.

WHY WORRY?

To close a menu without making a selection, click the menu name again or press Esc.

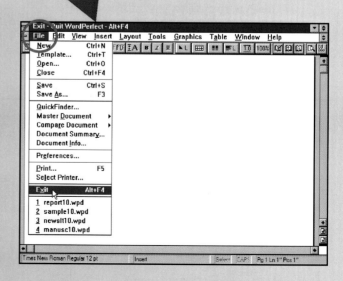

TASK 3

Displaying the Button Bar

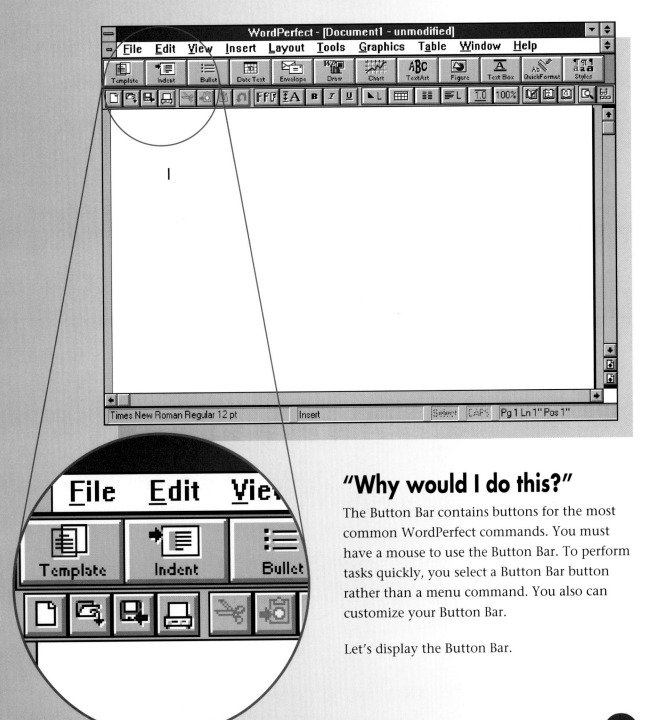

"Why would I do this?"

The Button Bar contains buttons for the most common WordPerfect commands. You must have a mouse to use the Button Bar. To perform tasks quickly, you select a Button Bar button rather than a menu command. You also can customize your Button Bar.

Let's display the Button Bar.

Task 3: Displaying the Button Bar

1 Point to **View** in the menu bar and click the **left mouse** button. This step opens the View menu. You see a list of View commands.

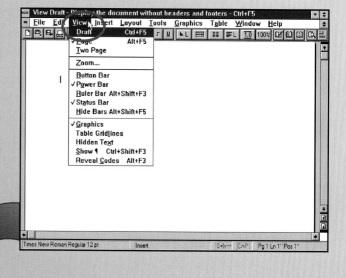

NOTE ▼

A check mark appears next to the menu command Button Bar in the View menu when the Button Bar is turned on.

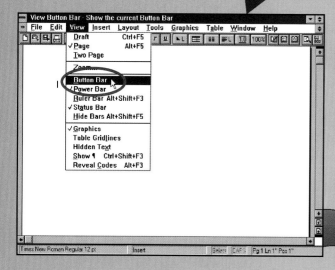

2 Point to **Button Bar** and click the **left mouse** button. This selects the Button Bar command.

NOTE ▼

To move the Button Bar, point somewhere on the bar where there isn't a button. The pointer changes to a hand. Drag the bar to its new location.

3 As you can see, the Button Bar appears on-screen. You can access commands (Indent, Bullets, and others) quickly from the Button Bar.

WHY WORRY?

The Button Bar command is a toggle. Select the command again to hide the Button Bar.

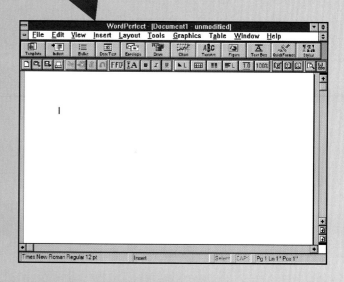

TASK 4
Hiding the Power Bar

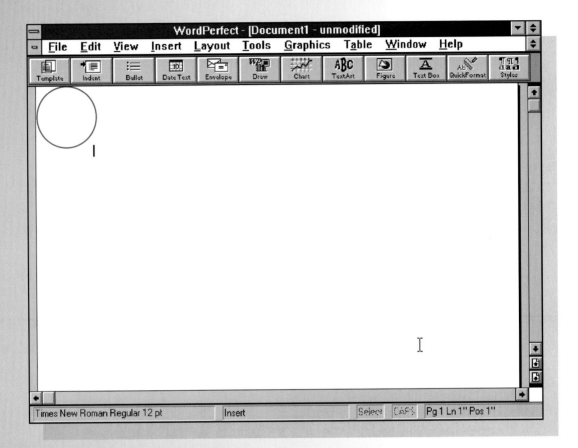

"Why would I do this?"

By default, the Power Bar appears at the top of the screen. But, perhaps you don't use the Power Bar, or you want to have a clean screen, or you want to make more lines of text in a document visible. You can hide the Power Bar to make more room on-screen.

Let's hide the Power Bar.

Task 4: Hiding the Power Bar

1 Point to **View** in the menu bar and click the **left mouse** button. This step opens the View menu. You see a list of View commands.

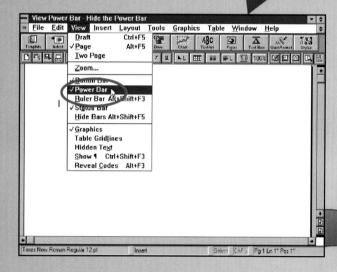

2 Point to **Power Bar** and click the **left mouse** button. This step selects the Power Bar command.

3 As you can see, the Power Bar is hidden.

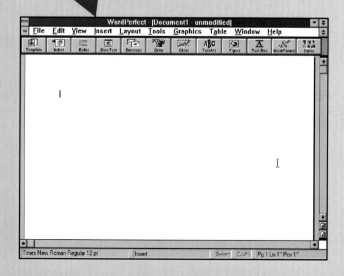

Displaying the Ruler Bar

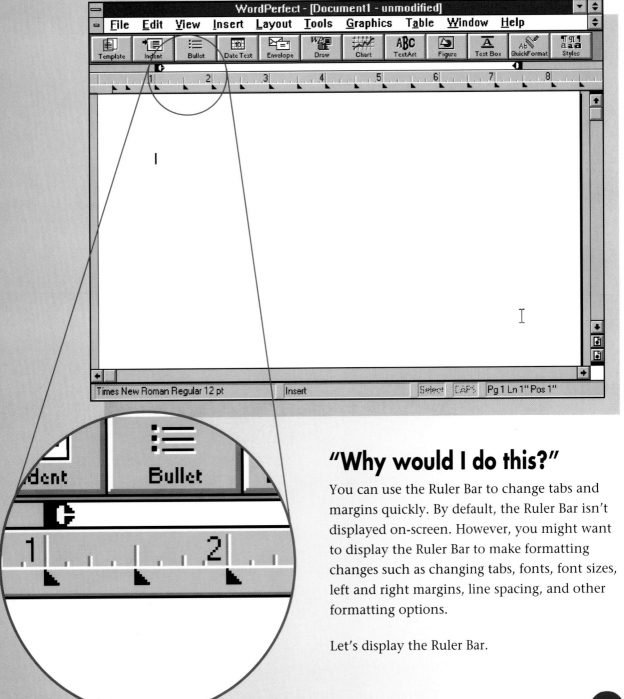

"Why would I do this?"

You can use the Ruler Bar to change tabs and margins quickly. By default, the Ruler Bar isn't displayed on-screen. However, you might want to display the Ruler Bar to make formatting changes such as changing tabs, fonts, font sizes, left and right margins, line spacing, and other formatting options.

Let's display the Ruler Bar.

Task 5: Displaying the Ruler Bar

1 Point to **View** in the menu bar and click the **left mouse** button. This step opens the View menu. You see a list of View commands.

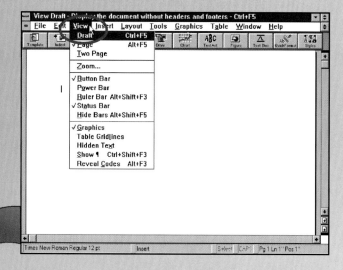

2 Point to **Ruler Bar** and click the **left mouse** button. This step selects the Ruler Bar command.

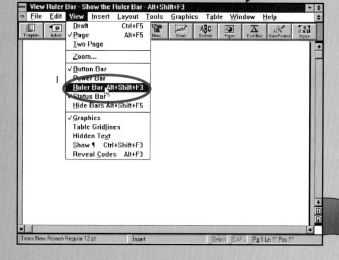

NOTE ▼

As a shortcut, you also can press Alt+Shift+F3 to display/hide the Ruler Bar.

3 As you can see, the Ruler Bar appears on-screen.

WHY WORRY?

The Ruler Bar command is a toggle. Select the command again to hide the Ruler Bar.

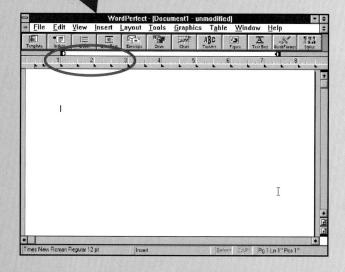

Getting Help

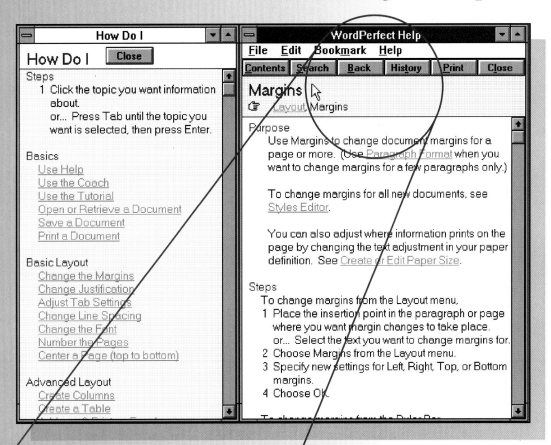

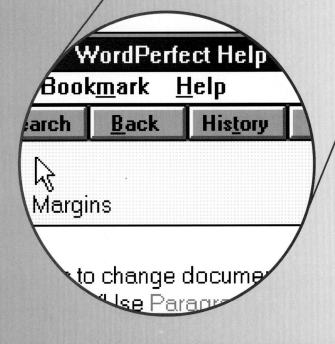

"Why would I do this?"

WordPerfect offers many ways to get help, and the Help feature has its own menu system. WordPerfect's How Do I feature provides specific procedures on how to use commands and functions, and perform operations in your WordPerfect documents.

Let's get some help on how to change margins.

Task 6: Getting Help

1 Click **Help** in the menu bar. Then click **Contents**. This step selects the Help Contents command. The Help window opens, and the name of the Help window appears in the title bar.

NOTE ▼

Help also is available through some WordPerfect commands that use a dialog box. Remember that any new command that is followed by an ellipsis (…) displays a dialog box.

2 Point to **How Do I** and click the **left mouse** button. This step selects the Help feature and displays a list of topics.

NOTE ▼

When the mouse pointer is on a topic for which you can get help, the pointer changes to a hand with a pointing finger.

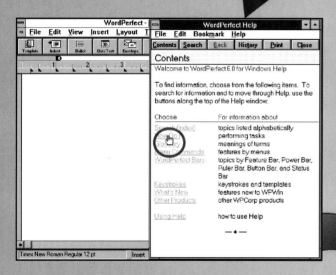

3 Point to the topic **Change the Margins** and click the **left mouse** button. This step displays help on margins.

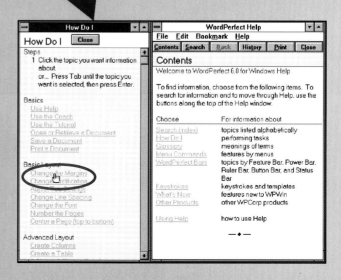

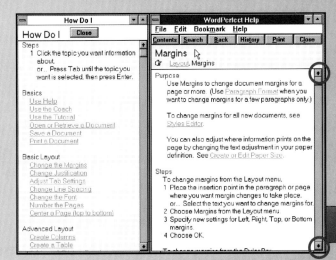

4 You can scroll this window, by clicking the scroll arrows.

5 After you read the explanation, click **File** in the Help window's menu bar. This step opens the File menu. Then, click **Exit**. This selects the File Exit command, and then closes the Help window.

WHY WORRY?

To quickly shut the WordPerfect Help window, double-click the Control menu box. This box is the small bar to the left of the window's title bar.

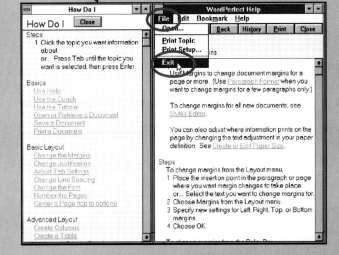

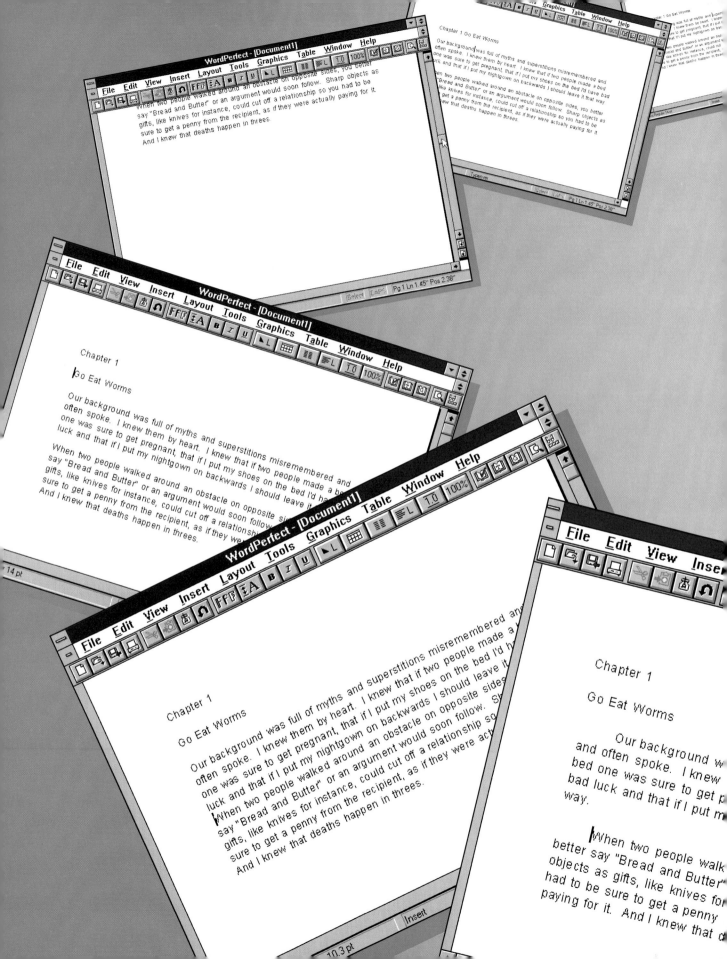

PART II
Entering and Editing Data

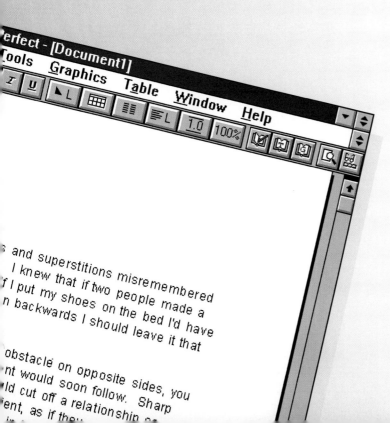

Any time you open up a document to continue work on it, you're adding to it. You can add text to existing text with some simple editing features. These features include Insert mode and Typeover mode. This part discusses both modes for adding text.

To add text to any document, you can either type in new text, cut and paste text from another document, or even merge another text file with the current one (it's called inserting a file).

The document is usually much larger than one screen can possibly display at one time. To place text in other areas of the document, you must be able to move to the desired locations. There are many ways to move around the document. You can use the arrow keys to move one character at a time. You can also use key combinations to quickly move around the document.

With WordPerfect's Go To command you can jump to a specific page that is out of view.

You can navigate around the document with the following arrow keys and key combinations:

To Move	Press
Right one character	→
Left one character	←
Up one line	↑
Down one line	↓
To the previous word	**Ctrl+←**
To the next word	**Ctrl+→**
To the beginning of a line	**Home**
To the end of a line	**End**
To the beginning of the document (before any codes)	**Ctrl+Home**
To the end of the document (after any codes)	**Ctrl+End**
To the previous screen	**PgUp**
To the next screen	**PgDn**

For information on other navigation keys, refer to your WordPerfect for Windows documentation. In this part, we will also show you how to move around the document quickly with the mouse.

After you enter data, you can type over text, insert a blank line, combine paragraphs, insert a tab, and insert page breaks.

This part also shows you how to select (or highlight) text, defining a portion of text that you want to overtype, delete, move, copy, edit, or enhance. WordPerfect highlights text you select.

You can select text with the following key combinations:

To Select	Press
One character to the right of the insertion point	**Shift**+ →
One character to the left of the insertion point	**Shift**+ ←
One line above the insertion point	**Shift**+↑
One line below the insertion point	**Shift**+↓
From the insertion point to the end of the line	**Shift**+**End**
From the insertion point to the beginning of the line	**Shift**+**Home**

To deselect text by using the keyboard, press any of the respective arrow keys.

You also can use the Edit Select command to quickly select a sentence, a paragraph, a page, or all the text in your document.

For information on other selection keys, refer to your WordPerfect for Windows documentation. In this part, we will also show you how to select text quickly with the mouse.

In this part, you learn how to delete text, undelete text, copy text, move text to other locations in the document, and undo mistakes.

The tasks that you learn in Part II will save you much time and effort when entering and editing text into your documents.

Adding Text

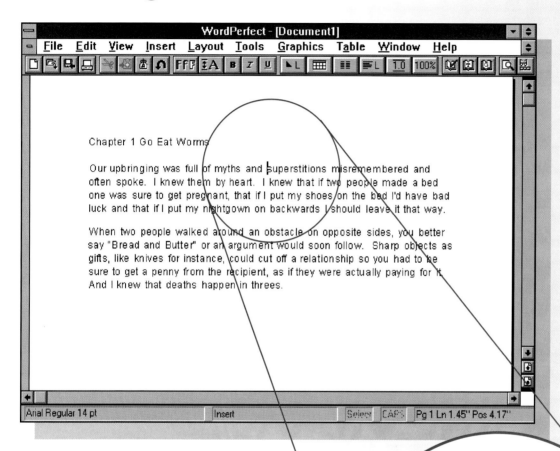

"Why would I do this?"

Normally, WordPerfect is in Insert mode. In Insert mode, you type text at the insertion point and the existing text moves forward to make room for the new text. In WordPerfect for Windows, you may find that you need to change a document by adding or replacing text after the document is complete.

In the following task, first hide the Ruler Bar; then display the Power Bar. That way, you can use the Power Bar tools at any time during the exercises. Then, enter text for the first chapter of a manuscript, and finally, insert additional text.

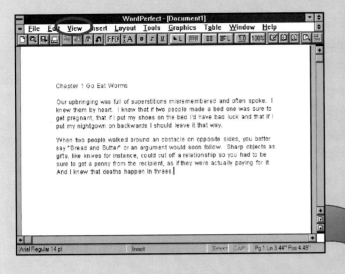

1 First, click **View**, and then click **Ruler Bar** to hide the Ruler Bar. Then, click **View** in the menu bar, and click **Power Bar** to display the Power Bar. Next, type the text that appears in the figure so that your computer screen matches the screen in the book.

NOTE ▼

The text on your screen and the text on the screen in this book might not match exactly because of the printer that you select.

2 Click before the word *superstitions*. This places the insertion point where you want to insert text. You can place the insertion point by clicking the location or by using the arrow keys.

WHY WORRY?

If you make a mistake when typing text, use the Backspace key or Delete key to correct the entry.

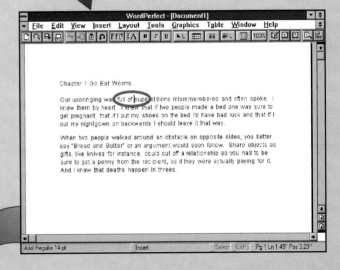

3 Type **myths and**. Then, press the **space bar**. This inserts the new text you type, moves the existing text to the right, and inserts a space between the new text and the original text.

NOTE ▼

Do not press the Insert key to insert text. Pressing the Insert key puts WordPerfect in Typeover mode.

TASK 8
Typing Over Text

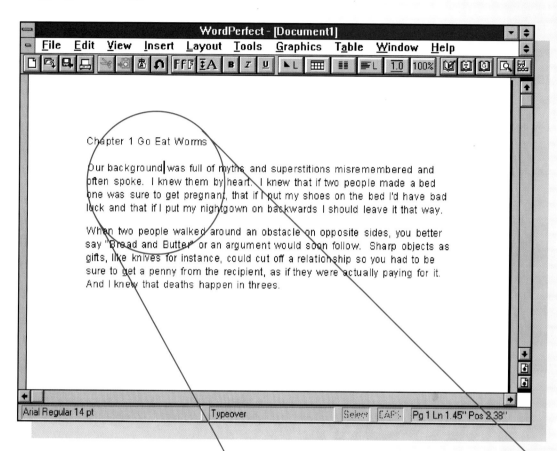

File   Edit   View   Insert   Layout   Tools   Graphics   Table   Window   Help

Chapter 1 Go Eat Worms

Our background was full of myths and superstitions misremembered and often spoke. I knew them by heart. I knew that if two people made a bed one was sure to get pregnant, that if I put my shoes on the bed I'd have bad luck and that if I put my nightgown on backwards I should leave it that way.

When two people walked around an obstacle on opposite sides, you better say "Bread and Butter" or an argument would soon follow. Sharp objects as gifts, like knives for instance, could cut off a relationship so you had to be sure to get a penny from the recipient, as if they were actually paying for it. And I knew that deaths happen in threes.

Arial Regular 14 pt   Typeover   Select CAPS Pg 1 Ln 1.45" Pos 2.38"

"Why would I do this?"

Typing over text means replacing the existing text with new text. Typing over text is handy when you want to correct typing errors or when you've typed the wrong text.

In your manuscript, type over the word *upbringing* with the word *background*.

apter 1 Go Eat Worms

Our background was full of r
often spoke. I knew them by
one was sure to get pregnan
uck and that if I put my nigh

en two people walked
read and Butter"

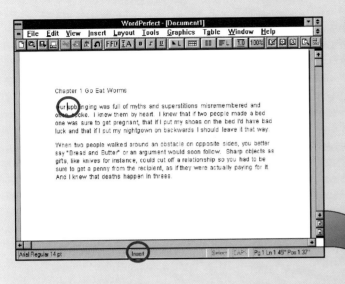

1 Click before the *u* in *upbringing*. This places the insertion point where you want to type over text. You can place the insertion point by clicking the location or by using the arrow keys.

2 Press **Insert**. This step puts WordPerfect in Typeover mode. The indicator Typeover appears in the status bar at the bottom of the screen. This mode types over rather than inserts text.

NOTE ▼

Be careful that you don't type over text that you want to keep.

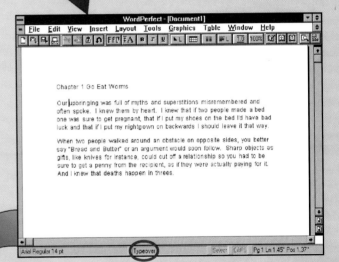

3 Type **background**; then, press **Insert**. WordPerfect deletes the original text and replaces it with *background*. The Insert key is a toggle. You press this key one time to turn on Typeover mode; press it again to turn off Typeover mode.

WHY WORRY?

To reverse the change, click the Undo button on the Power Bar immediately after you overwrite the text.

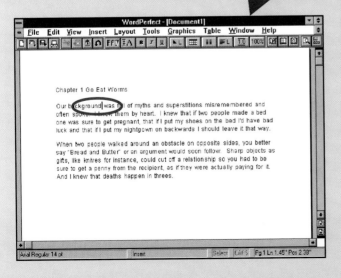

TASK 9
Moving Around the Document

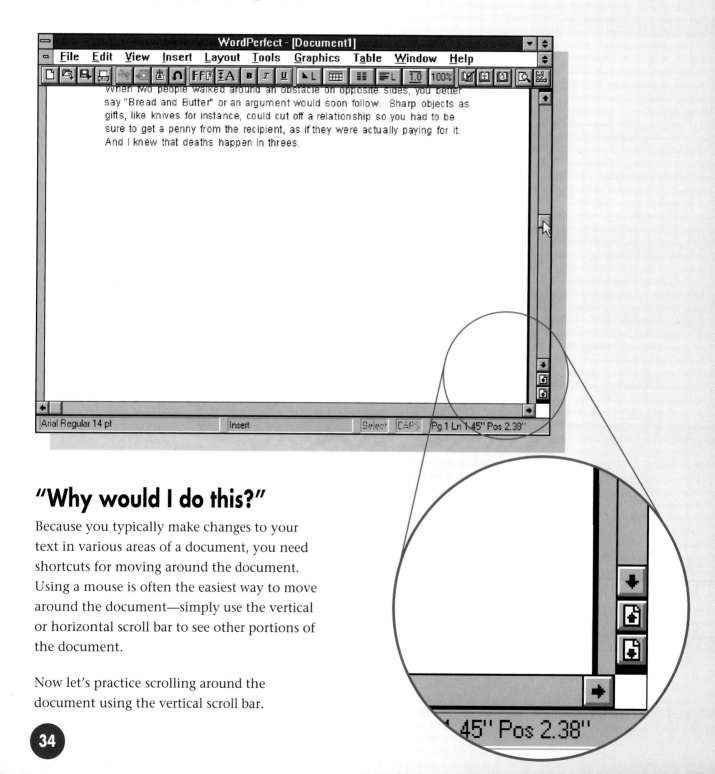

"Why would I do this?"

Because you typically make changes to your text in various areas of a document, you need shortcuts for moving around the document. Using a mouse is often the easiest way to move around the document—simply use the vertical or horizontal scroll bar to see other portions of the document.

Now let's practice scrolling around the document using the vertical scroll bar.

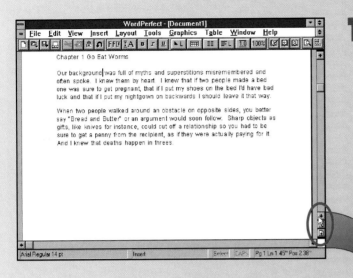

1 Click four times on the down scroll arrow at the bottom of the vertical scroll bar. Clicking the down scroll arrow moves the document down one or more lines at a time, depending on the length of the document.

NOTE ▼

To scroll the document continuously in a particular direction, you point to the up, down, left, or right scroll bar arrow and hold down the mouse button.

2 Click three times on the up scroll arrow at the top of the vertical scroll bar. Clicking the up scroll arrow scrolls the document up one or more lines at a time, depending on the length of the document.

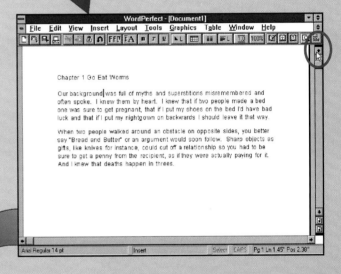

3 Click halfway down in the vertical scroll bar. Clicking in the scroll bar moves the document up or down one window length at a time. Notice that the scroll box is now near the bottom of the vertical scroll bar.

Task 9: Moving Around the Document

4 To drag the scroll box, point to the scroll box with the mouse, click and hold down the mouse button, and move the mouse pointer to the top of the vertical scroll bar. Dragging the scroll box moves the document quickly to a new location in the direction of the scroll box.

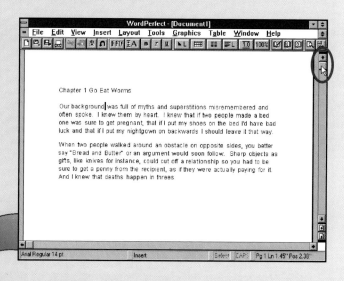

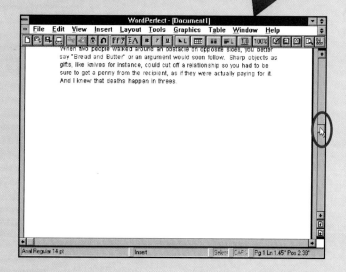

5 Drag the scroll box to the middle of the vertical scroll bar. WordPerfect moves the document down on-screen and displays the end of the document.

NOTE ▼

Keep in mind that whatever scroll bar action you perform on a vertical scroll bar can be performed the same way on the horizontal scroll bar.

WHY WORRY?

If you run out of room to move the mouse on your desktop or mouse pad, just lift the mouse and then put it down in a different place.

Inserting a
Blank Line

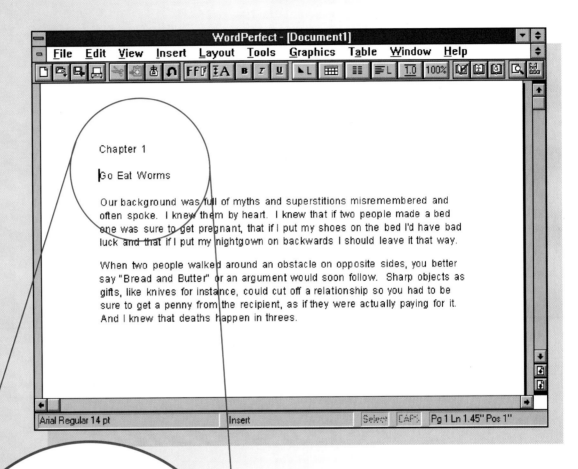

"Why would I do this?"

Unlike typing on a typewriter, you don't have to press Enter at the end of each line. When text reaches the end of the line, WordPerfect automatically wraps the text to the next line. You press Enter to enter a hard return at the end of a short line, to insert a blank line between paragraphs, or to end a paragraph.

Let's enter a hard return to end a paragraph, and then enter another hard return to insert a blank line.

Task 10: Inserting a Blank Line

1 Press **Ctrl+Home** to move to the top of the document. Click after *Chapter 1*. This step places the insertion point where you want to insert a blank line. Be sure to click after the *1*.

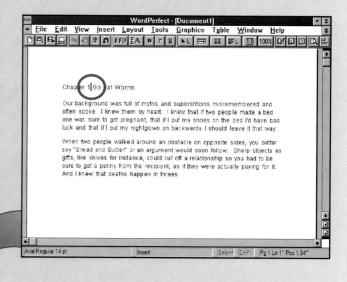

2 Press **Enter**. Pressing Enter ends the current paragraph. When you press Enter, WordPerfect inserts a hard return code in the document.

> **NOTE** ▼
>
> By default, codes do not appear on-screen. If you want to display codes, click View in the menu bar and choose Reveal Codes, or press Alt+F3.

3 Press **Enter**. Then, press **Delete** to delete the extra space. This step inserts a blank line. The first two lines of text are now separated by a blank line.

> **NOTE** ▼
>
> A hard return forces a line break. If you add or delete text, the hard return stays in the same position in the text. When you add or delete text, WordPerfect automatically readjusts the wrap or flow of the paragraph.

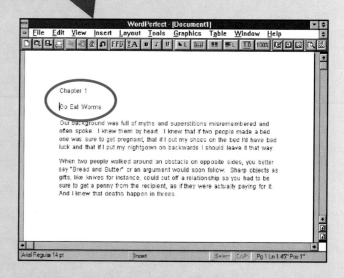

Combining Paragraphs

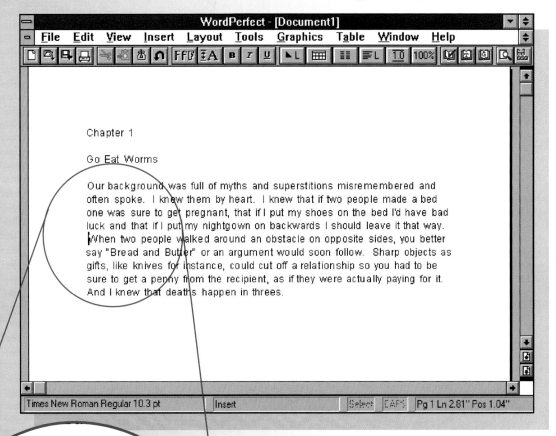

Chapter 1

Go Eat Worms

Our background was full of myths and superstitions misremembered and often spoke. I knew them by heart. I knew that if two people made a bed one was sure to get pregnant, that if I put my shoes on the bed I'd have bad luck and that if I put my nightgown on backwards I should leave it that way. When two people walked around an obstacle on opposite sides, you better say "Bread and Butter" or an argument would soon follow. Sharp objects as gifts, like knives for instance, could cut off a relationship so you had to be sure to get a penny from the recipient, as if they were actually paying for it. And I knew that deaths happen in threes.

Our background
often spoke. I kne
one was sure to ge
luck and that if I put
When two people w
say "Bread and But
gifts, like knives fo
sure to get a pen
And I knew th

"Why would I do this?"

Sometimes, you might delete text within a paragraph and find that the remaining text in that paragraph should be combined with the text in the next paragraph. In WordPerfect, you can easily combine paragraphs by deleting the hard returns between paragraphs and inserting space between sentences.

Let's combine two paragraphs.

Task 11: Combining Paragraphs

1 Click after *way.* at the end of the first paragraph. This places the insertion point at the end of the first paragraph. Be sure to click after the period.

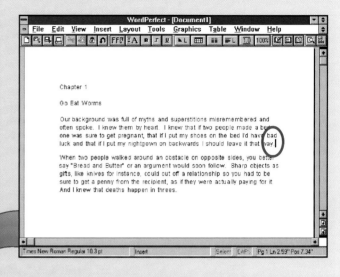

2 Press **Delete**. Pressing the Delete key deletes the hard return at the end of the current paragraph.

3 Press **Delete** again. Then, press the **space bar** twice. Pressing the Delete key again deletes the blank line between the paragraphs. The second paragraph moves up next to the first paragraph. Pressing the space bar twice inserts two spaces between the two sentences.

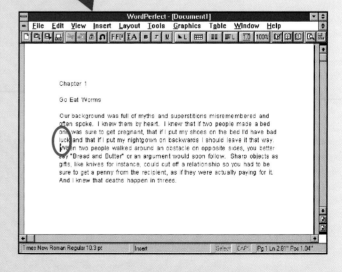

Inserting a Tab

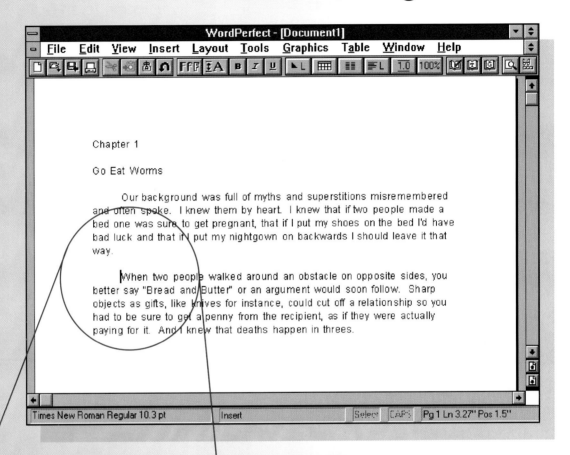

Chapter 1

Go Eat Worms

Our background was full of myths and superstitions misremembered and often spoke. I knew them by heart. I knew that if two people made a bed one was sure to get pregnant, that if I put my shoes on the bed I'd have bad luck and that if I put my nightgown on backwards I should leave it that way.

When two people walked around an obstacle on opposite sides, you better say "Bread and Butter" or an argument would soon follow. Sharp objects as gifts, like knives for instance, could cut off a relationship so you had to be sure to get a penny from the recipient, as if they were actually paying for it. And I knew that deaths happen in threes.

"Why would I do this?"

Just like typing on a typewriter, you press the Tab key to insert a tab. Perhaps you want to insert a tab at the beginning of a paragraph to indent the text from the left margin. You might want to use tabs in a memo heading to insert space between the heading and the memo information.

Let's insert a tab at the beginning of the paragraph.

Task 12: Inserting a Tab

1 Click before *Our* in the first sentence. The insertion point is where you want to insert a tab (at the beginning of the paragraph).

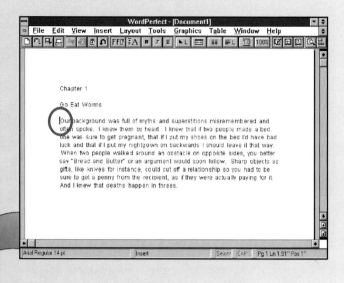

2 Press **Tab**. Pressing Tab inserts a tab and moves the insertion point to the next tab stop. As you can see, the first sentence begins at the tab stop. WordPerfect provides a default tab stop every 1/2 inch. You can also change the tab settings.

> **NOTE** ▼
>
> When you press the Tab key, WordPerfect inserts a tab code in the document. By default, tab codes do not appear on-screen. If you want to see the tab codes, press Alt+F3.

3 Click after *way*. Be sure to click after the period. Press **Enter** twice to end the first paragraph and insert a blank line.

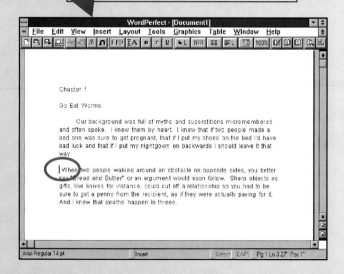

4 Press **Delete**. This step removes the unwanted space.

5 Press **Tab** to insert a tab. The first sentence in the paragraph begins at the tab stop.

NOTE ▼

To indent an entire paragraph from the left margin, use Indent.

WHY WORRY?

Press Backspace to delete the Left Tab code.

TASK 13
Inserting a Page Break

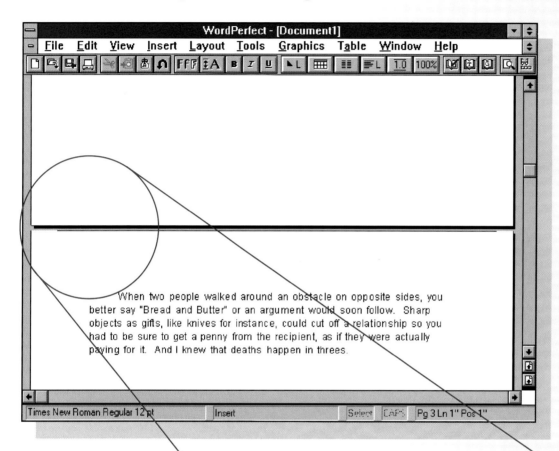

When two people walked around an obstacle on opposite sides, you better say "Bread and Butter" or an argument would soon follow. Sharp objects as gifts, like knives for instance, could cut off a relationship so you had to be sure to get a penny from the recipient, as if they were actually paying for it. And I knew that deaths happen in threes.

"Why would I do this?"

When you have entered enough text to fill a page, WordPerfect automatically inserts a soft page break. When you make changes, Word-Perfect adjusts the locations of the soft page breaks. However, you can insert hard page breaks where you want one page to end and another page to begin. This feature is useful if you want to create a title page, or separate a table or graphics from paragraphs of text.

Insert a page break at the end of the chapter. Then, insert another page break below the second paragraph.

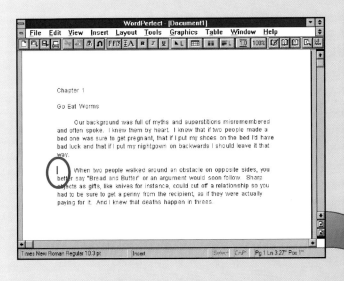

1 Click before the tab (blank space) at the beginning of the second paragraph. This step places the insertion point where you want the new page to begin. Remember that you can place the insertion point by using the mouse or the arrow keys.

2 Press **Ctrl+Enter** to insert a hard page break in the document. Because the View mode is set to Page view, a break in the paper appears. In Draft View mode, a thick line appears. When you print the document, a new page will begin where you inserted the page break.

On-screen, a soft page break appears as a single dashed line.

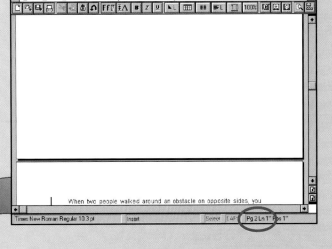

3 Click at the beginning of the blank line below the second paragraph. This places the insertion point where you want another new page to begin. Then, press **Ctrl+Enter**. Pressing Ctrl+Enter inserts a hard page break in the document.

WHY WORRY?

To combine pages, click View in the menu bar and choose Reveal Codes. Click the Hpg code in the Codes window and press Delete.

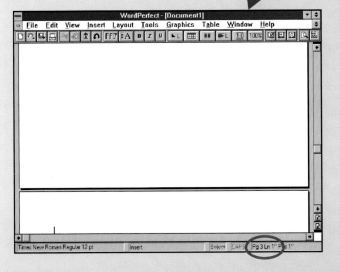

Going to a Specific Page

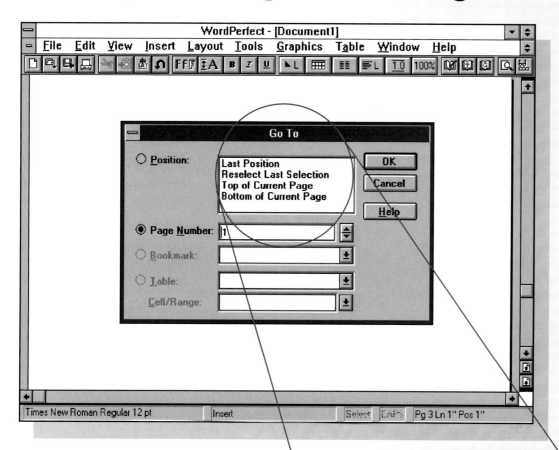

"Why would I do this?"

The Go To command is useful for quickly moving through pages in a document, especially longer ones. You can jump to any page that is out of view in the current document. Perhaps you're working on page 3 and you want to make a change on page 1.

Move to page 1 using the Go To command.

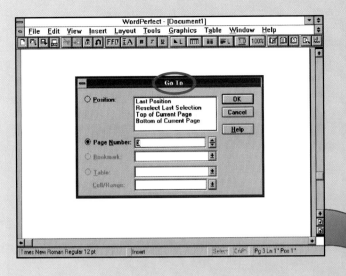

1 Press **Ctrl+G**. Ctrl+G is the Go To key. Pressing Ctrl+G selects the Edit Go To command. WordPerfect opens the Go To dialog box. The insertion point is in the Page Number text box. The current page number is listed in this box.

2 Type **1**. Typing 1 tells WordPerfect to go to page 1.

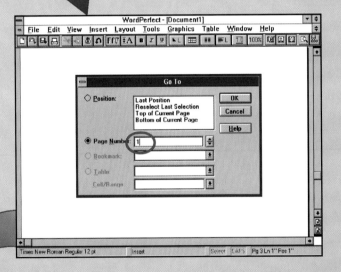

3 Press **Enter**. This confirms the command. WordPerfect moves the insertion point to page 1.

WHY WORRY?

To return to the previous position, select the Edit Go To command. Click the Position option button. Then click Last Position. Finally, click OK.

Selecting Text

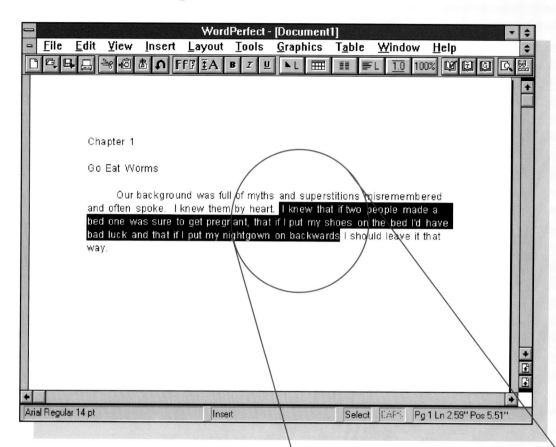

"Why would I do this?"

Knowing how to select text is essential because most of the commands and options in WordPerfect operate on the selected text. You can select any amount of text, a block of text, a word, a sentence, and a paragraph with the mouse. For example, you may want to boldface a title or a heading.

Select a section of text with the mouse. Next, select a word, then a sentence, a paragraph, and a block of text.

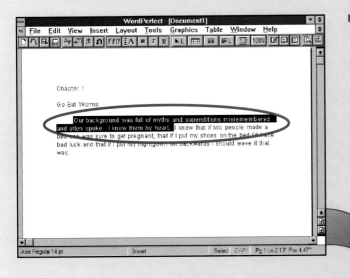

1 Place the mouse pointer in front of *Our background* and click and hold down the left mouse button. Then move the mouse pointer to after *I knew* in the sentence *I knew that if two*. Clicking at the beginning of the text you want to select, holding down the left mouse button, and dragging the mouse pointer across the text you want to select highlights the amount of text you specify.

2 Double-click the word *background*. This step selects a word.

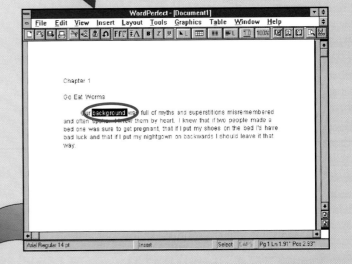

3 Triple-click the mouse anywhere within the sentence. This selects a sentence.

4 Click the mouse four times anywhere within the paragraph. This selects a paragraph.

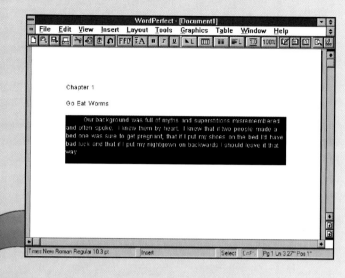

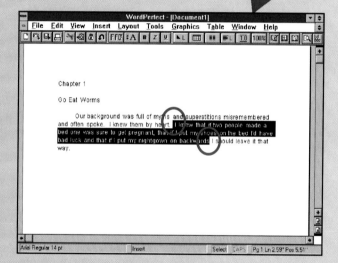

5 Position the mouse pointer at the beginning of the text you want to select, click the left mouse button, and then hold down **Shift** as you click the end of the block of text.

WHY WORRY?

To deselect text, simply click anywhere outside the selected text.

Deleting Text

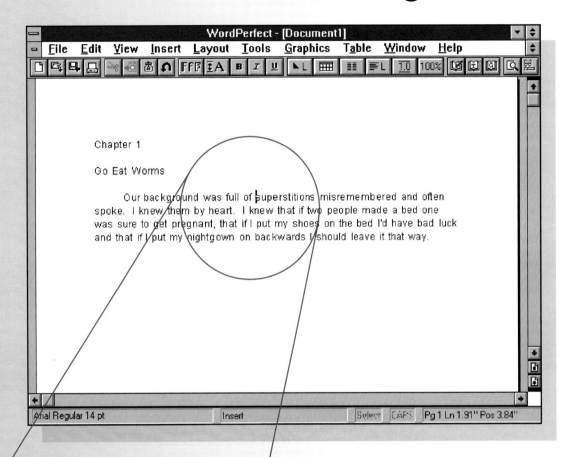

"Why would I do this?"

Sometimes text you initially typed into the document needs to be changed. Instead of over-writing the incorrect text, you can select any amount of text and then press the Delete key.

To delete just one character, use the Delete or Backspace key. The Delete key deletes the character to the right of the insertion point; the Backspace key deletes the character to the left of the insertion point.

In the manuscript, let's assume the words *myths and* in the first sentence on page 1 are incorrect. We will delete this text.

Task 16: Deleting Text

1 Click before the *m* in *myths,* hold down the mouse button, and drag across the word *myths* and the next word *and.* This step selects *myths and,* the text you want to delete.

2 Press **Delete**. WordPerfect deletes the text. The remaining text moves up to fill in the gap.

3 Click the **Undo** button (the button that contains an arrow that curves to the left and down) in the Power Bar. The entry you just deleted is restored.

WHY WORRY?

You also can use Edit Undelete to restore deleted text.

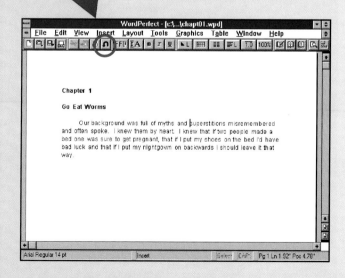

Undeleting Text

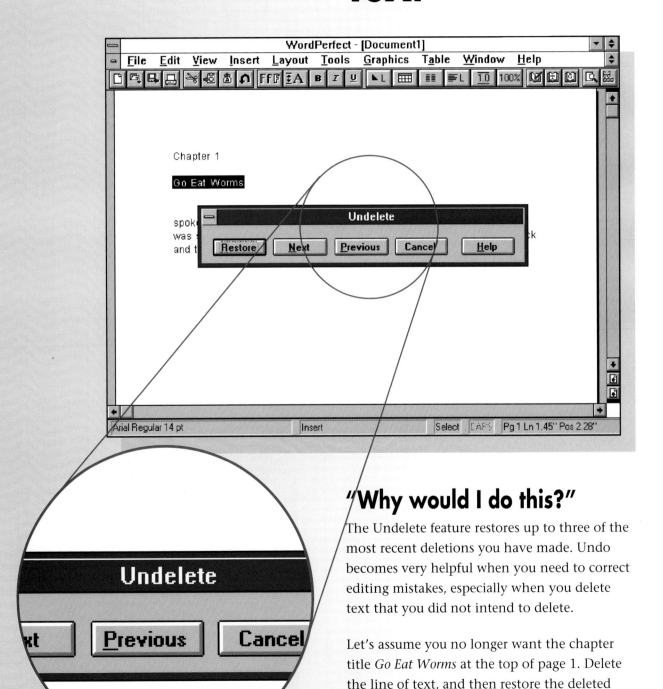

Chapter 1

Go Eat Worms

"Why would I do this?"

The Undelete feature restores up to three of the most recent deletions you have made. Undo becomes very helpful when you need to correct editing mistakes, especially when you delete text that you did not intend to delete.

Let's assume you no longer want the chapter title *Go Eat Worms* at the top of page 1. Delete the line of text, and then restore the deleted text by using the Undelete feature.

Task 17: Undeleting Text

1 Press **Ctrl+Home** to move to the top of the document. Click before the *G* in *Go Eat Worms* and drag across the chapter title. Then, press **Delete**. This deletes the line of text. This is the deleted text you want to restore with Undelete.

2 Click **Edit** in the menu bar. Then, click **Undelete**. This selects the Edit Undelete command. You see the Undelete dialog box. You can use this box to cycle through up to three previous deletions. The text you want to restore is the most recent deletion and appears in the document. This text is highlighted. Click **Restore**.

WHY WORRY?

Click Cancel to cancel the operation. The text remains deleted.

3 This selects the Restore button and restores the text to the document.

NOTE ▼

You also can use Edit Undo to restore text. You must use this command immediately after you delete the text—before you perform any other operation. You can only restore the most recent deletion when you use Edit Undo.

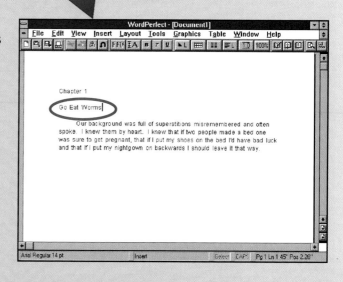

TASK 18
Copying Text

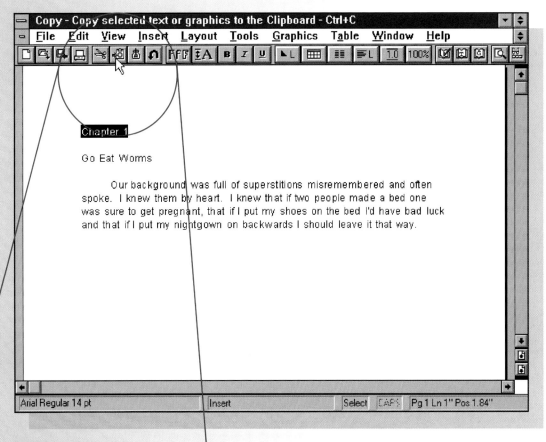

"Why would I do this?"

You can save the time of retyping information in the document by copying text over and over again. For example, you might want to copy a paragraph from one page to another page. That way you wouldn't have to type the paragraph over again, saving you time and keystrokes.

Using the manuscript you've created, let's copy the chapter name *Chapter 1* to the top of page 3. You can use the Copy and Paste buttons to quickly copy the line of text to the new location.

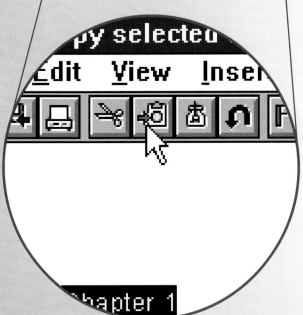

Task 18: Copying Text

1 Click before the *C* in *Chapter 1* and drag across the chapter title. This selects the text you want to copy—in this case, Chapter 1.

NOTE ▼

To copy text using drag-and-drop editing, select the text. Click and hold down the Ctrl key and the mouse button. You see a white piece of paper and a black piece of paper above the mouse pointer. Drag the text to the new location. Release the Ctrl key and the mouse button.

2 Click the **Copy** button (the button that contains a clipboard with a yellow circle and an arrow pointing to the right) in the Power Bar. Clicking the Copy button copies the text to the Clipboard. The Clipboard is a temporary holding area for text and graphics.

3 Scroll down to page 3 and click the blank line at the top of the page. This step places the insertion point where you want the copied text to appear.

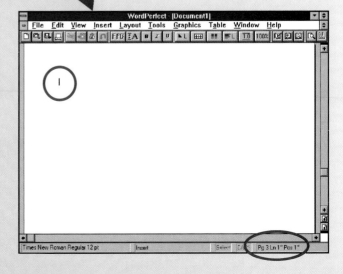

4 Click the **Paste** button (the button that contains a paste jar) in the Power Bar. Clicking the Paste button selects the Paste command. The copied text now appears in the new location (as well as the original location).

NOTE ▼

You also can use the Ctrl+C and Ctrl+V key combinations to select the Copy and Paste commands.

5 Click before the *1* in *Chapter 1*. Press **Insert**, type **2**, and press **Insert** again. This step changes the chapter number.

WHY WORRY?

If you copied the wrong text or copied the data to the wrong location, click the Undo button in the Power Bar to undo the most recent copy. Then start over. Or, just delete the misplaced text.

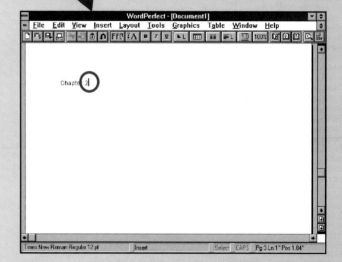

Moving Text

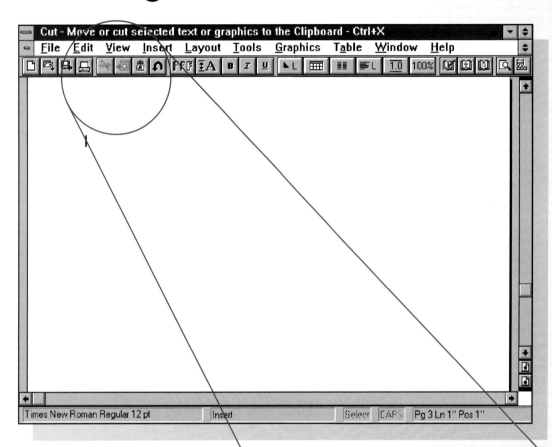

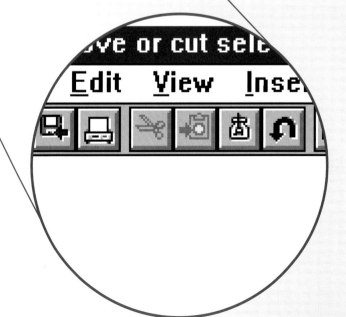

"Why would I do this?"

The Move command lets you remove information from one location in the document and place it in another location. You do not have to go to the new location and enter the same text and then erase the text in the old location.

Suppose we want to move *Chapter 2* above the paragraph on page 2. Let's use the Cut and Paste buttons in the Power Bar to move our paragraph.

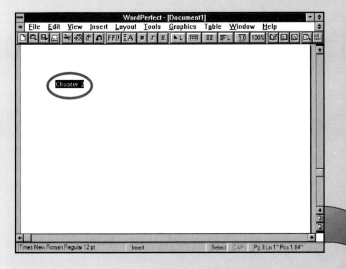

1 On page 3, click before the *C* in *Chapter 2* and drag across the chapter title. This step selects the text you want to move.

> **NOTE** ▼
>
> To move text using drag-and-drop editing, simply select the text, drag it to the new location, then release the mouse button.

2 Click the **Cut** button (the button that contains scissors) in the Standard toolbar. Clicking the Cut button cuts the text from the document and places it on the Clipboard (a temporary holding area).

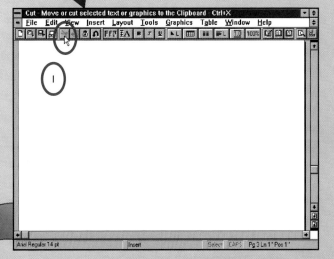

3 Click before the tab (the blank space) in the paragraph on page 2. This step places the insertion point where you want to move the text.

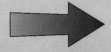

Task 19: Moving Text

4 Click the **Paste** button (the button that contains a paste jar) in the Power Bar to paste the text in the new location.

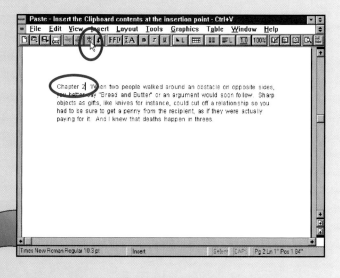

NOTE ▼

You also can use the Ctrl+X and Ctrl+V key combinations to select the Cut and Paste commands.

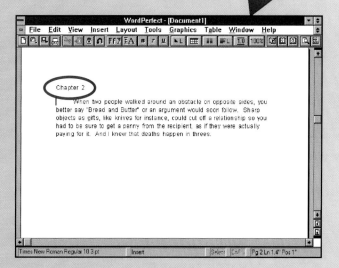

5 The text now appears in the new location (but not in the original location).

WHY WORRY?

If you moved the wrong text or moved the text to the wrong location, click the Undo button in the Power Bar to undo the most recent move. Then start over.

Undoing Changes

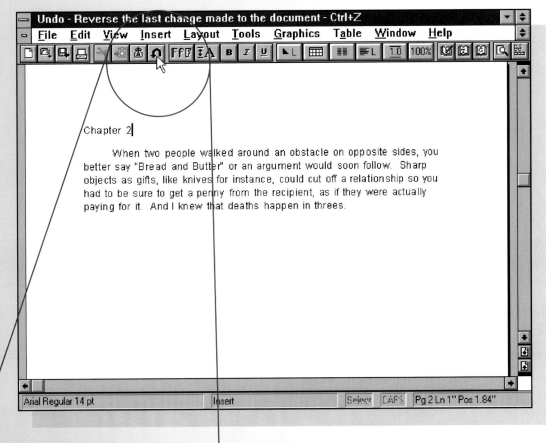

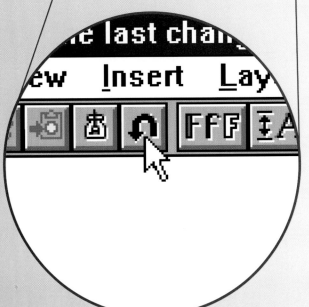

"Why would I do this?"

The Undo feature recovers the most recent changes to document text. For instance, if you edit the document and make a mistake, you can use Undo to reverse the last editing command you performed. Undo becomes very helpful when you need to correct editing and formatting mistakes, especially when you delete text that you did not intend to delete.

Let's assume you no longer want the words *Chapter 2* at the top of page 2. You will delete the line of text. Then, it's easy to change your mind—you can restore the deleted text by using the Undo feature.

Task 20: Undoing Changes

1 On page 2, click before the *C* in *Chapter 2* and drag across the chapter title. Then, press **Delete**. This step deletes the line of text. This is the deleted text you want to restore with Undo.

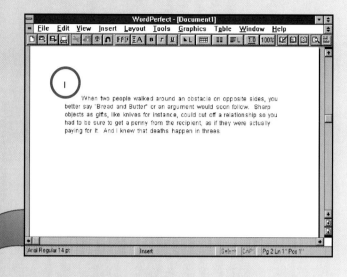

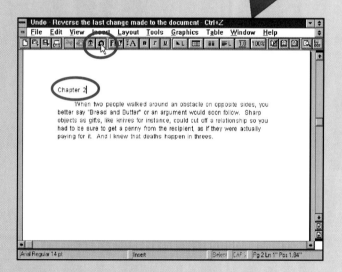

2 Click the **Undo** button (the button that contains an arrow that curves to the left and down) in the Power Bar. Clicking the Undo button selects the Undo command. WordPerfect restores the deleted text. As you can see, the document returns to its preceding form.

NOTE ▼

You also can press Ctrl+=Z to select the Edit Undo command.

WHY WORRY?

Click the Undo button a second time in the Power Bar to "undo" the Undo.

PART III

Managing Files

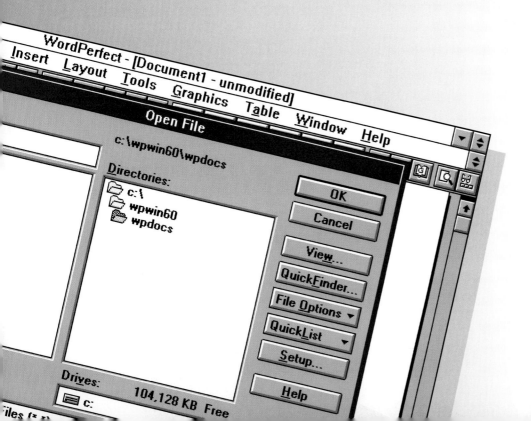

Part III: Managing Files

This part gives you details about managing document files in WordPerfect. You learn how to save your work, abandon a document, close a document, open a document, and create a new document.

By default, Timed Backup is turned on and saves a backup copy of your document every 10 minutes. You can specify the directory in which you want to save the backup files. To do so, choose the File Preferences command, double-click on the File icon, and specify the directory in which you want to save the backup files. WordPerfect saves the backup files with a .BK! extension. Timed backups can protect you from data loss due to power failures by saving a backup copy of your on-screen document to disk.

It is a good idea to save your file every 5 or 10 minutes. If you don't save your work, you could lose it. Suppose that you have been working on a document for a few hours and your power goes off unexpectedly—an air conditioning repairman at your office shorts out the power, a thunderstorm hits, or something else causes a power loss. If you haven't saved, you lose all your hard work. Of course, you also should make backup copies on floppy disks from time to time.

When saving files, use only alphanumeric characters in the file name, don't use spaces or punctuation marks and type either upper- or lowercase characters. You do not have to retype an extension. WordPerfect automatically adds the .WPD extension. If you don't specify where the document is stored to, WordPerfect stores it in the C:\WPWIN60\WPDOCS directory. The C:\WPWIN60\WPDOCS directory is automatically set up when you install WordPerfect.

Saving a file that you previously saved is slightly different from saving a newly created document. When you save a document you saved before, you save the current version on-screen and overwrite the original disk version. This means you always have the most current version of your file stored on disk.

If you want to keep both versions—the on-screen version and the original— you can use the File Save As command to save the on-screen version with a different name. Saving a file with a new name gives you two copies of the same document with differences in their data. When you save a file with a new name, you also can save the file in a different directory or drive.

WordPerfect also lets you close a previously saved document without saving the changes. Or if you create a new document and you don't want to keep it, WordPerfect lets you abandon the document. That way, you can close the new document, choose not to save the changes, and discard the document.

You can open more than one document at a time. For example, you might have two separate documents that contain related information. While using one document, you can view the information in another.

When you open several documents, they can begin to overlap and hide documents beneath other documents. WordPerfect lets you rearrange the documents so that some part of each document is visible. Arranging the open windows into smaller windows of similar sizes is called *tiling*. The Tile feature is handy when you want to copy or move text between two documents side by side. You can use the Window Tile command to arrange the windows into smaller windows.

You also can arrange document windows so that the window you want to view is not overlapped by other windows. This method keeps all the windows the same size, but stair-steps each window into a layered effect. The term for this method is *cascading*. You can use the Window Cascade command to arrange the windows into a layered effect.

If you want to display one document after you are finished using the tile or cascade window arrangement, close the documents you do not want displayed and click the maximize button in the document's window. The document you want to display fills the screen.

In this part, you are introduced to the essential file management skills you need to work in WordPerfect.

TASK 21
Saving a Document

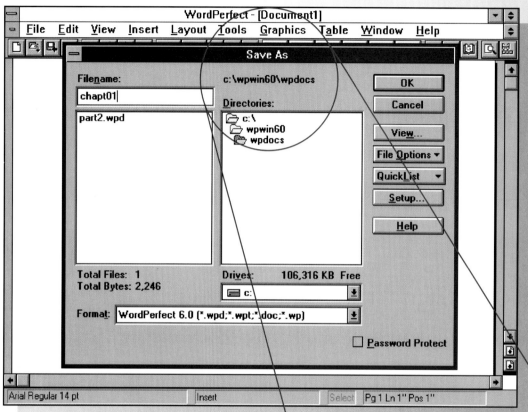

"Why would I do this?"

Until you save the document, your data is
not stored on disk. You can lose your data if
something happens, such as a power loss. When
you need the document again, you can retrieve
it from the disk. Save your work every 5 or 10
minutes and at the end of a work session. Then
close the document if you want to clear the
screen.

Now save the document you have been working
on in the previous tasks. Name the file
CHAPT01.

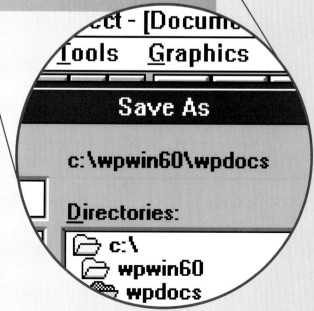

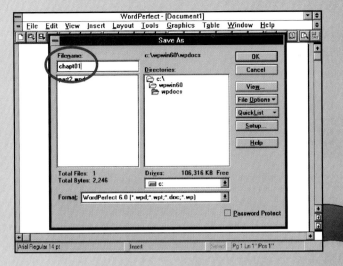

1 Click the **Save** button in the Power Bar. Clicking the Save button selects the Save command. The first time you save the document, WordPerfect displays the Save As dialog box. Type **CHAPT01** in the Filename text box. CHAPT01 is the file name you want to assign to the document. You can type as many as eight characters.

NOTE ▼

The Save As dialog box lists current directories and the current drive.

2 Click **OK**. This accepts the file name and returns you to the document. The file name, CHAPT01.WPD, appears in the title bar. WordPerfect automatically adds the WPD extension. If you have not made any changes, the word *unmodified* appears after the file name.

WHY WORRY?

If you type a file name that already exists, WordPerfect displays an alert box that asks `File already exists. Do you want to replace it?` Click Cancel to return to the Save As dialog box, and then type a new name.

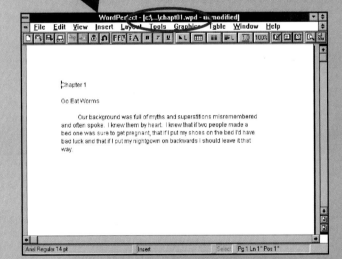

Closing a Document

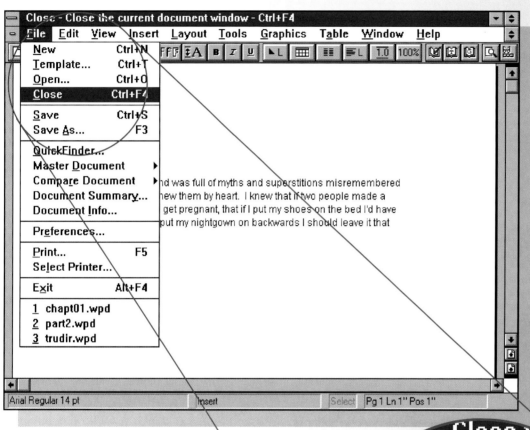

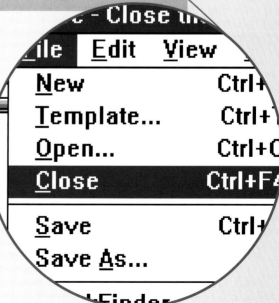

"Why would I do this?"

When you no longer want to work with a document, you can use the File Close command to close the document. You then can go on to another document or exit WordPerfect.

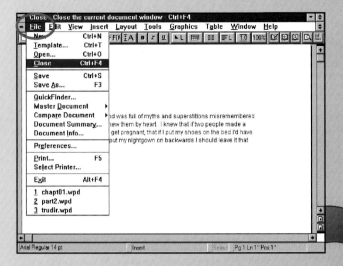

1 Click **File** in the menu bar. This opens the File menu. You see a list of File commands.

NOTE ▼

You also can use the Control menu box in the upper left corner of the document window on the left end of the menu bar to close the file—simply double-click the Control Menu box.

2 Click **Close**. This selects the File Close command. WordPerfect closes the document. From here, you can open a document or create a new document.

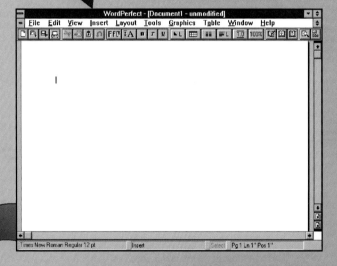

3 If you have made changes, WordPerfect displays an alert box that reminds you to save the changes. Choose **Yes** to save the changes and close the document, or choose **No** to ignore the changes and close the document.

WHY WORRY?

If you decide that you do need to make changes, click Cancel in the alert box.

TASK 23
Opening an Existing Document

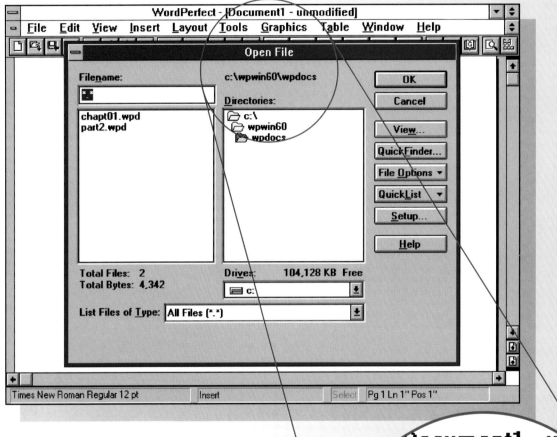

"Why would I do this?"

After you save a document, you can view it again or make changes to it later. You can have up to nine documents open at once.

Suppose you want to work with the CHAPT01 file again. Use the Open button on the Power Bar to open the closed document file.

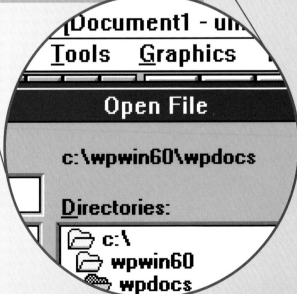

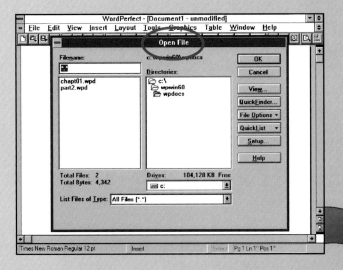

1 Click the **Open** button in the Power Bar. Clicking the Open button selects the File Open command. You see the Open File dialog box. The insertion point is in the Filename text box.

NOTE ▼

The Open File dialog box also contains the Filename list and the Directories list. If the file is stored in a different directory, double-click the directory name in the Directories list. To move up a directory level, double-click [. .].

2 If necessary, click the down scroll arrow in the Filename list to find the CHAPT01.WPD file. When you see the file, double-click it. This selects the file and opens the document. WordPerfect displays the document on-screen. The file name appears in the title bar.

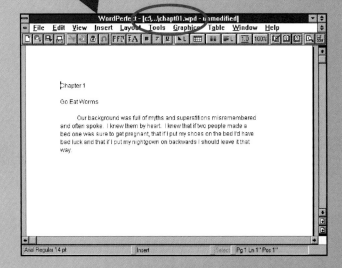

NOTE ▼

You can type the file name if you know it, or you can use the mouse or the arrow keys to select the file name in the Filename list.

WHY WORRY?

If you open the wrong document, close the document and try again.

TASK 24
Creating a New Document

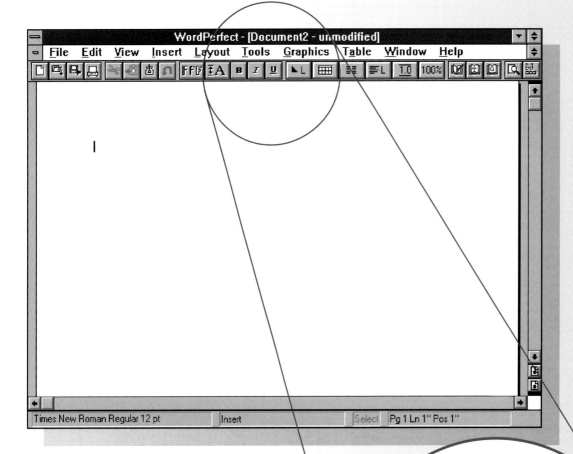

"Why would I do this?"

WordPerfect presents a new, blank document when you first start the program. You can create another new document at any time. Perhaps you have closed and saved the active document and want to begin a new one.

Let's create a new document and see how it works. Then you can abandon the new document.

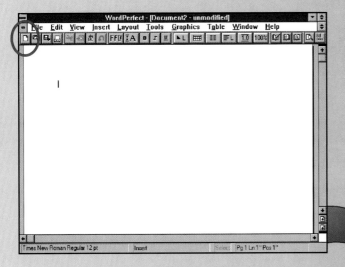

1 Click the **New Document** button in the Power Bar. Clicking the New Document button selects the File New command. A blank document appears on-screen. This document is titled DOCUMENT2 (the number varies depending on the number of documents you have open).

NOTE ▼

When you start WordPerfect, the program automatically displays a blank document. You don't have to use the File New command in this case.

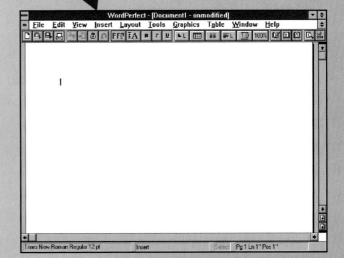

2 Click **File** in the menu bar and then click **Close**. This selects the File Close command. WordPerfect closes the document.

WHY WORRY?

If you don't want to create a new document, abandon the document. Just close the document without saving changes.

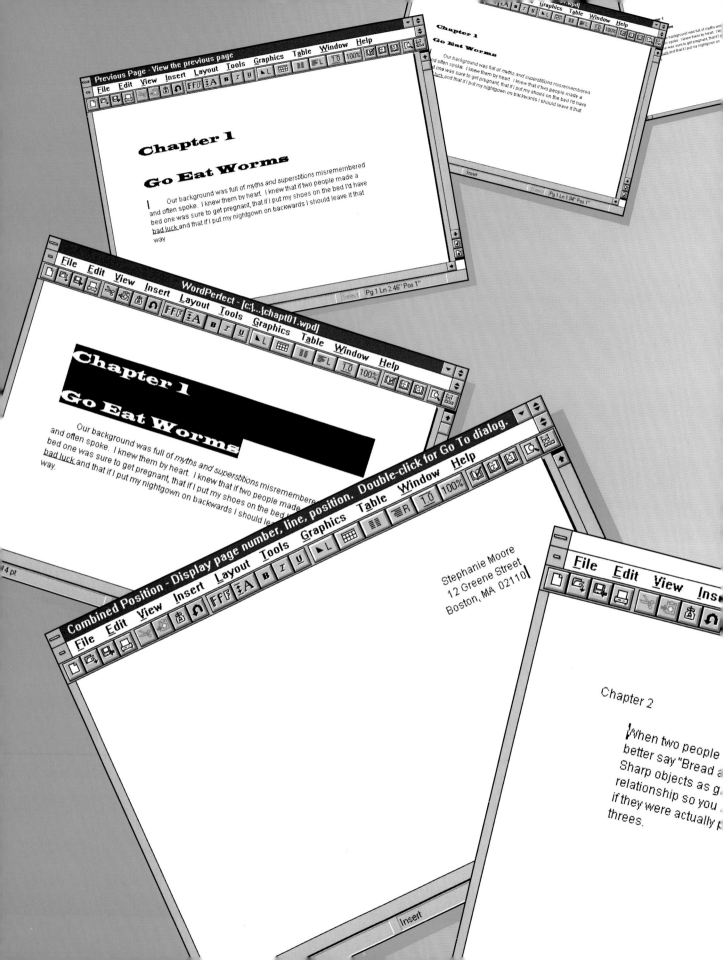

PART IV

Formatting Your Document

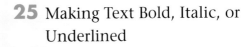

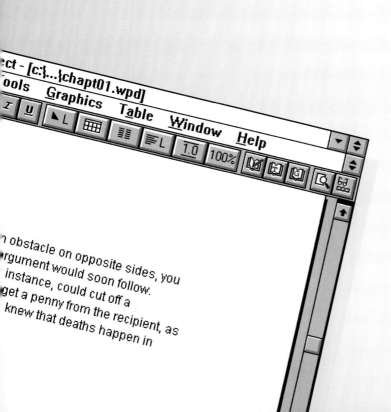

n obstacle on opposite sides, you
rgument would soon follow.
instance, could cut off a
get a penny from the recipient, as
knew that deaths happen in

Formatting the document means you can change the appearance of text in your document. With WordPerfect's formatting tools, you can make your document more attractive and readable. In this part you learn how easy it is to boldface, italicize, and underline text; you learn how to change the font, change the font size, center and right-align text. You also learn how to indent text, create a hanging indent, create a bulleted list and a numbered list, set tabs, and double-space a document.

typestyle

italic

bold

underline

The Underline command enables you to underline text in your document. To underline text, you can use the Layout Font command and then choose from several underline styles in the Font dialog box. The Underline styles include underline, double underline, underline spaces, and underline tabs. In this part, you learn how to apply the underline style using the mouse.

Changing the font and the font size is an easy way to change the look and feel of your document. A *font* is a style of type in a particular typeface and size. WordPerfect displays various fonts and font sizes in the Formatting toolbar. You can use the fonts provided by WordPerfect as well as fonts designed especially for your printer. If WordPerfect does not have a screen version of the printer font you select, it substitutes a font. In this case, the printout looks different from the screen.

You can apply fonts to a single word or to any amount of text you want to change. You also can change the font size and font colors. The Font Color options in the Font dialog box let you easily change font colors. There are many font colors in various shades, hues, and patterns that you can choose to make your document more attractive. Of course, you must have a color monitor and a color printer to benefit from changing font colors.

You can align text left, right, center, full, or all. The default alignment is Left. Left alignment means that text is aligned flush with the left margin. Right-aligned text appears flush with the right margin; center alignment centers text between the left and right margins. Full alignment spreads text between the left and right margins by expanding or contracting the space between words. If the last line of text is shorter than the rest of the lines, WordPerfect does not justify the last line of text. All justification is the same as full justification, except that the last line in a paragraph is spread between the left and right margins.

Left-aligned text appears "ragged right" on the page or column, which is warm and readable. Usually, left alignment is used for conventional and office correspondence. Full-justified text, which has an orderly look, is generally used in multiple-column newsletters, newspapers, and magazines.

WordPerfect provides another way to align paragraphs. You can indent paragraphs from the left, right, or both margins. You also can indent only the first line of the paragraph, or you can create a hanging indent.

Normally, documents are single-spaced. However, Word-Perfect enables you to change the line spacing in your documents. You can specify single, 1.5 lines, double, or specify the exact amount of line spacing you want.

In this part, you learn some of the most important formatting operations you need for changing the appearance of your documents.

TASK 25

Making Text Bold, Italic, or Underlined

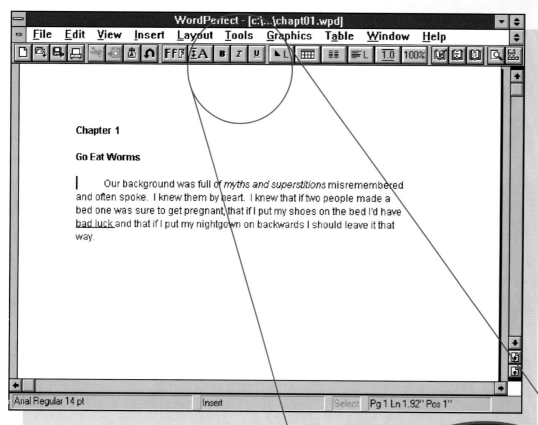

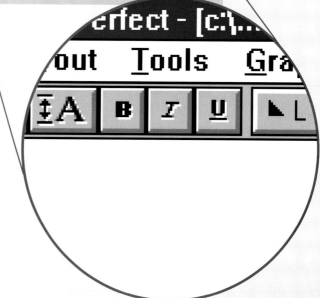

"Why would I do this?"

To bring attention to important text in a document, you can make text bold, italic, or underlined to emphasize significant words and phrases.

In your manuscript, the chapter titles *Chapter 1* and *Go Eat Worms* would look better in boldface. First, boldface the chapter titles; then, italicize the words *myths and superstitions* in the first sentence on page 1. Finally, underline the words *bad luck* in the last sentence on page 1.

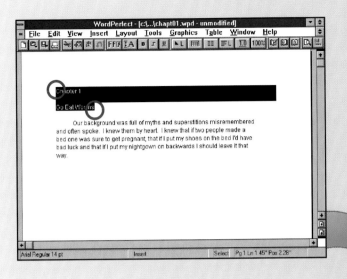

1 Click before the C in *Chapter 1* and drag down after the s in *Worms*. The two lines of the text you want to make bold are selected.

2 Click the **Bold Font** button (the button that contains a **B**) on the Power Bar. Clicking on the Bold Font button applies bold to the selected text—in this case, the chapter titles. To deselect the text, click outside it. Now you can see the boldfaced text.

NOTE ▼

You also can press Ctrl+B to select the Bold command.

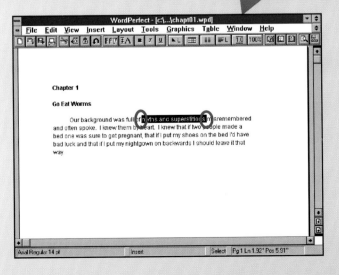

3 Click before the word *myths* and drag after the word *superstitions* to highlight the text you want to italicize.

Task 25: Making Text Bold, Italic, or Underlined

4 Click the **Italic Font** button (the button that contains an *I*) on the Power Bar. Clicking the Italic Font button italicizes the text—in this case, the words *myths* and *superstitions*. To deselect the text, click outside it. Now you can see the italicized text.

> **NOTE** ▼
> You also can press Ctrl+I to select the Italic command.

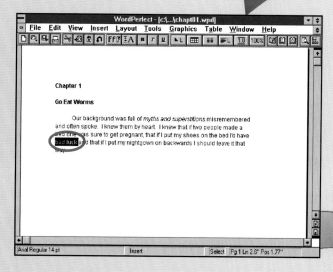

5 Click before the word *bad* and drag to the end of the next word, *luck*. The text you want to underline is selected.

> **WHY WORRY?**
> To undo the font style, click the Undo button on the Power Bar immediately. Or you can simply click on the Bold, Italic, or Underline button again to cancel the font style.

6 Click the **Underline Font** button (the button that contains a <u>U</u>) on the Power Bar. Clicking the Underline Font button underlines the text. Click outside the selected text to deselect it.

> **NOTE** ▼
> You also can press Ctrl+U to select the Underline command.

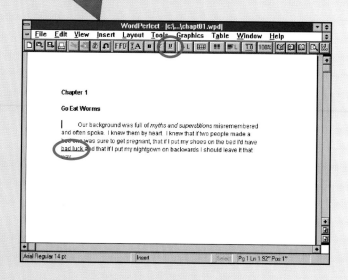

Changing the Font

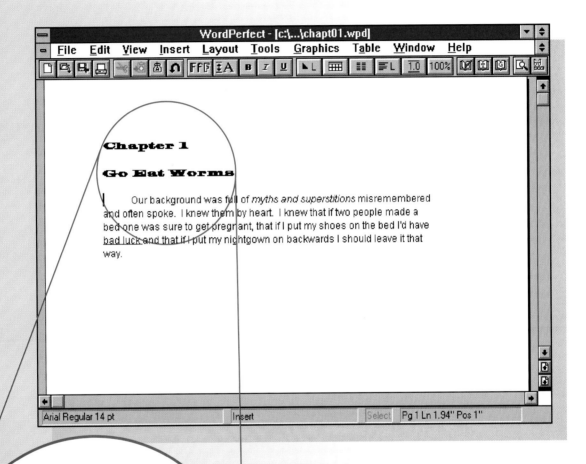

"Why would I do this?"

To draw attention to important words and phrases in a document, you can change the font in a document. You can change the font of a title to Wide Latin, for example, to enhance the text.

In your manuscript, let's change the font for the chapter titles.

Task 26: Changing the Font

1 Point in the left margin next to *Chapter 1*. The mouse pointer is an arrow pointing to the upper right. Now, drag down to the next line *Go Eat Worms*. The text you want to change is selected.

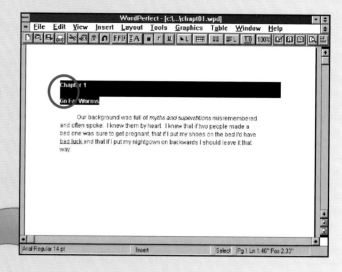

2 Click the **Font Face** button (the button that contains the letters FFF) on the Power Bar. This step displays the list of fonts. Click any font in the list. We chose Wide Latin. If you don't have this font, select one you do have. This step changes the font for the selected text.

3 Click outside the selected text to deselect the text. The text appears different from the way it was before.

WHY WORRY?

To undo the font change, immediately click the Undo button on the Power Bar.

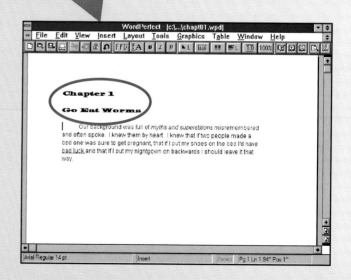

Changing the Font Size

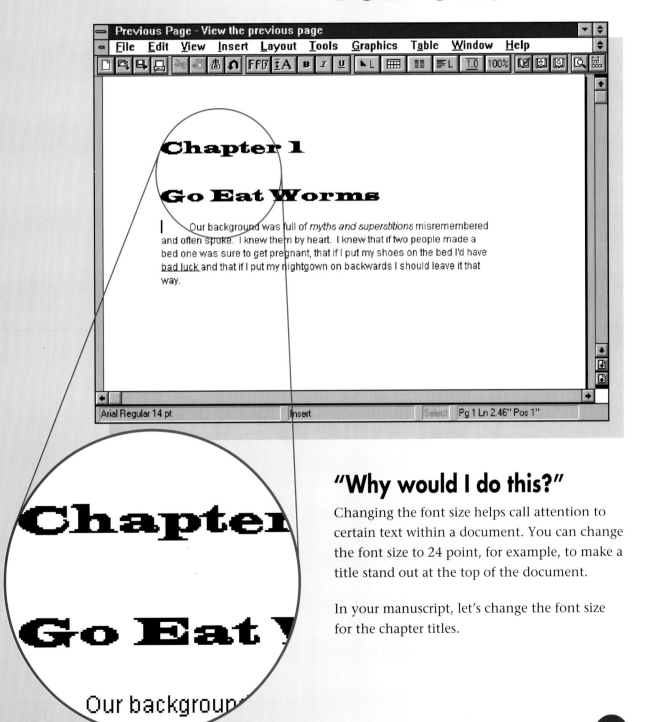

"Why would I do this?"

Changing the font size helps call attention to certain text within a document. You can change the font size to 24 point, for example, to make a title stand out at the top of the document.

In your manuscript, let's change the font size for the chapter titles.

Task 27: Changing the Font Size

1 Point in the left margin next to *Chapter 1*. The mouse pointer is an arrow pointing to the upper right. Now, drag down to the next line *Go Eat Worms*. The text you want to change is selected.

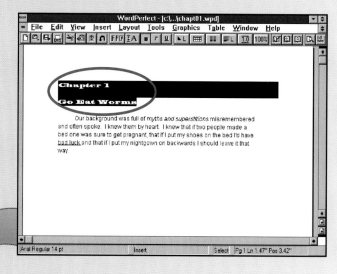

2 Click the **Font Size** button (the button that contains the letter A with a double-headed arrow) on the Power Bar. This displays the list of font sizes. Click a larger font size (a higher number). We chose 24. If you don't have this font size, select one that you do have.

NOTE ▼

The font sizes in the list can vary, depending on the type of printer you have and the selected font.

3 Click outside the selected text to deselect the text. The text appears bigger than it was before.

WHY WORRY?

To undo the font size change, immediately click the Undo button on the Power Bar.

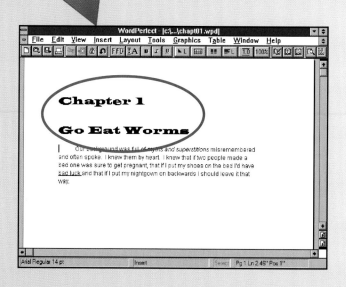

Centering Text

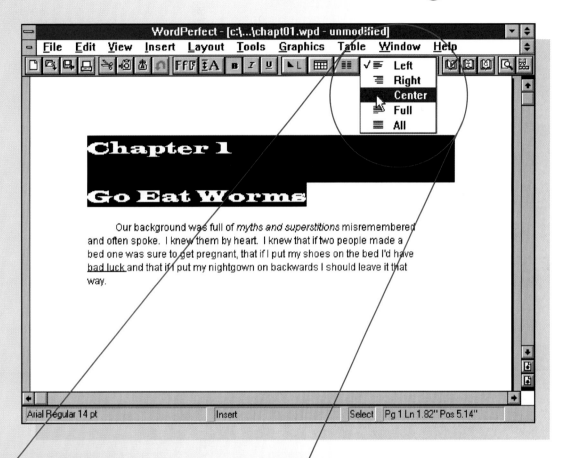

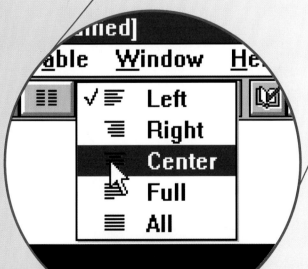

"Why would I do this?"

When you enter text into a document, text automatically aligns flush with the left margin. You can change the alignment of text at any time. For instance, you might want to center a title across the top of the document.

In your manuscript, the chapter titles are aligned left. These titles might look better if they were centered. Let's center the titles.

Task 28: Centering Text

1 Click the left margin next to *Chapter 1* and drag down to the next line *Go Eat Worms*. The text you want to center is selected.

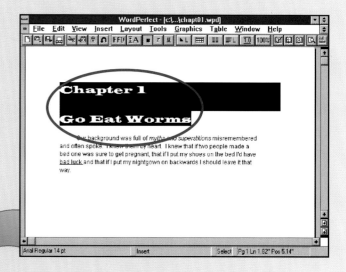

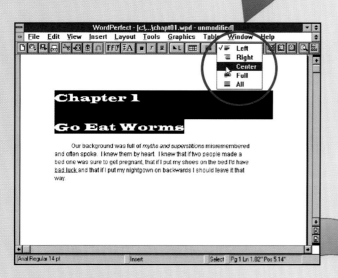

2 Click the **Justification** button (the button that contains several lines of text and a letter, usually the letter L) on the Power Bar, hold down the mouse button, and drag to the **Center** option. Then, release the mouse button. This selects the Center command. WordPerfect centers the text—in this case, the chapter titles.

NOTE ▼

You also can press Shift+F7 to center a line of text.

3 Click outside the selected text. This deselects the text.

WHY WORRY?

To undo the most recent alignment change, click the Undo button on the Power Bar immediately.

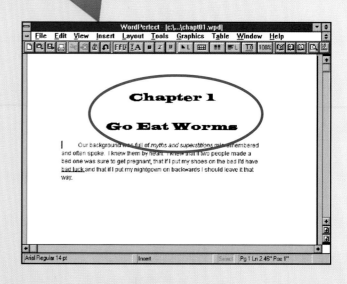

Aligning Text Flush Right

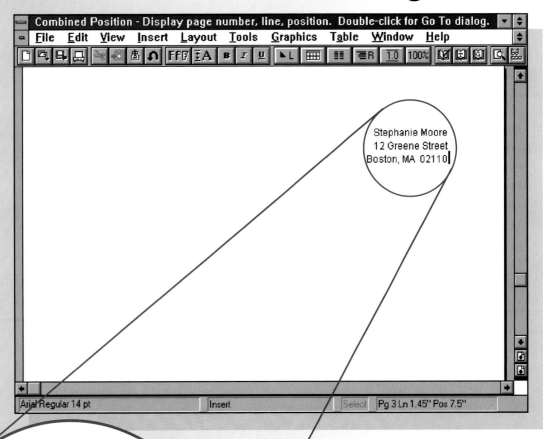

"Why would I do this?"

Aligning text to the right is used for special effects. For example, you might want to align the date in a letter flush right.

On page 3 in your manuscript, type the inside address for a letter. By default, this text will be aligned left. Align the text flush right.

Task 29: Aligning Text Flush Right

1 Press **Ctrl+End** to move the insertion point to page 3, the last page. Type the address that appears in the figure so that your screen matches the computer screen in the book. Select the three lines of text.

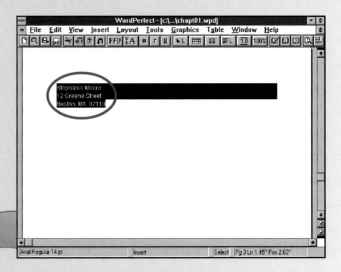

2 Click the **Justification** button (the button that contains several lines of text and a letter, usually the letter L) on the Power Bar, hold down the mouse button and drag to the **Right** option. Then, release the mouse button. This step selects the Right command. WordPerfect right aligns the address.

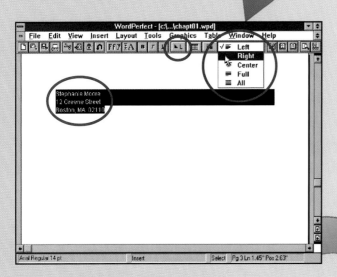

3 Click outside the selected text. This step deselects the text.

NOTE ▼

You also can press Alt+F7 to right-align text.

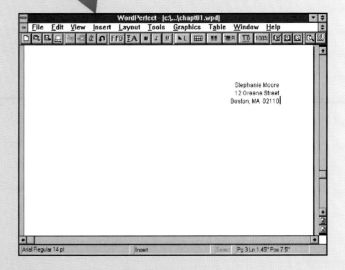

Indenting Text

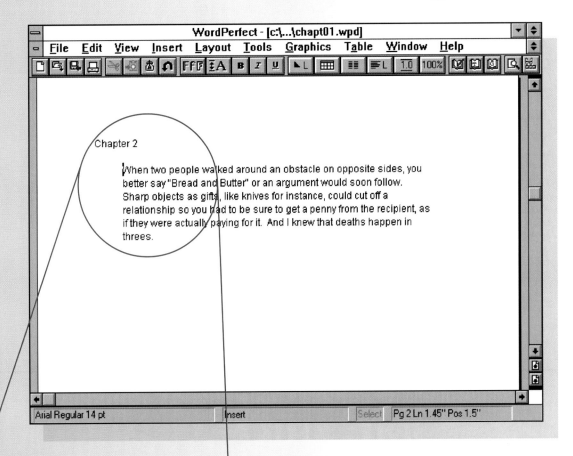

"Why would I do this?"

Another way to align paragraphs is to indent them relative to the margins. You can adjust the indents by specific measurements or by the Ruler. You might want to indent the entire paragraph to the right of the left margin to make the paragraph stand out from the rest of the paragraphs. A contract, for example, may contain indented paragraphs.

In your manuscript, remove the tab preceding the paragraph on page 2, and then indent the entire paragraph on page 2 to the right of the left margin by 1/2 inch.

Task 30: Indenting Text

1 Click before the tab (blank space) in the paragraph on page 2. Then, press **Delete** to remove the tab. As you can see, the insertion point is already in the paragraph you want to indent.

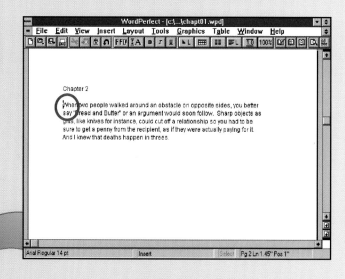

2 Click **Layout** in the menu bar, and then click **Paragraph**. You see a list of paragraph formatting options.

3 Click **Indent**. The current paragraph is indented from the left margin. The tab settings control how far the text indents. With the default settings, tabs are set every half inch, and the text is indented one-half inch.

> **NOTE** ▼
>
> You also can press F7 to indent the current paragraph 1/2 inch. To undo the indent, click the Undo button on the Power Bar immediately.

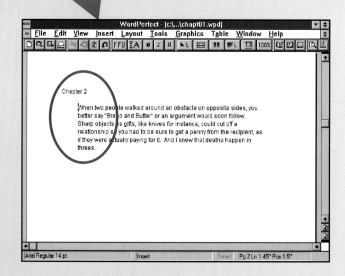

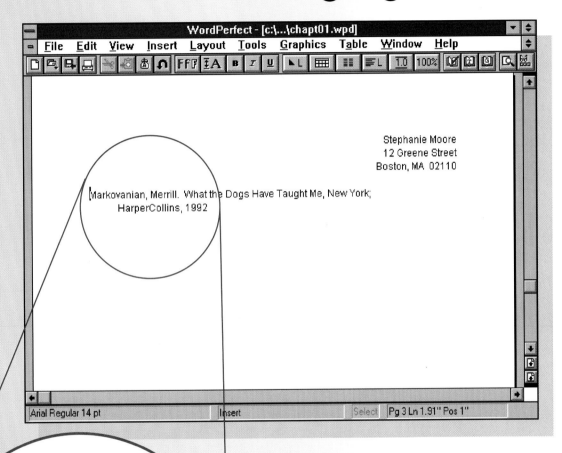

Creating a Hanging Indent

"Why would I do this?"

A *hanging indent* "hangs" the first line of a paragraph to the left of the rest of the paragraph. Hanging indents are useful for bulleted and numbered lists, glossary items, and bibliographic entries.

In your manuscript, first type a bibliographic entry on page 3, and then create a hanging indent for the paragraph.

Task 31: Creating a Hanging Indent

1 Press **Ctrl+End** to move to the last page, page 3. You will need to press **Enter** after the last line of the address and press **Enter** again. Then, you also need to change your justification to Left. Click at the beginning of the blank line below the address. and then type **Markovanian, Merrill. What the Dogs Have Taught Me, New York; HarperCollins, 1992.** Press **Enter** twice.

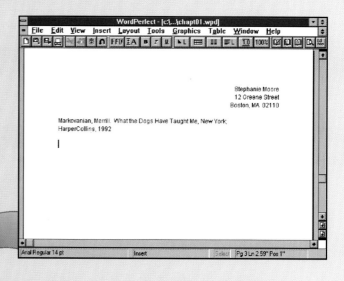

2 Click before the *M* in *Markovanian*. This step places the insertion point where you want to indent text.

> **NOTE** ▼
>
> This task creates a hanging indent for one paragraph. You also can create hanging indents for several paragraphs at one time. To create hanging indents for more than one paragraph, select those paragraphs.

3 Click **Layout** in the menu bar. You see a list of Layout commands.

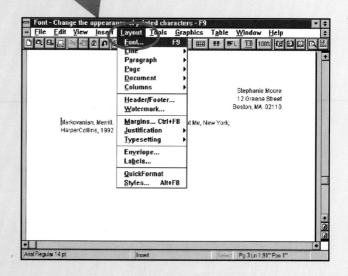

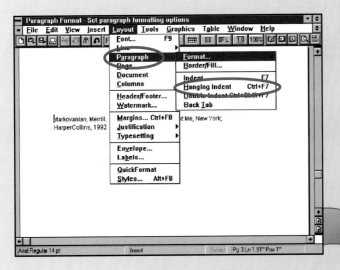

4 Click **Paragraph**. You see a list of paragraph formatting options. Click **Hanging Indent**.

5 The first line of the paragraph is flush left, but the second line is indented 1/2 inch (provided you are using the default tab settings).

NOTE ▼

You also can press Ctrl+F7 to create a hanging indent.

WHY WORRY?

If you've made other changes since creating the hanging indent, you can undo the change by deleting the indent code. Press Alt+F3 to display Reveal Codes; then delete the Hd Left Ind and Hd Back Tab codes.

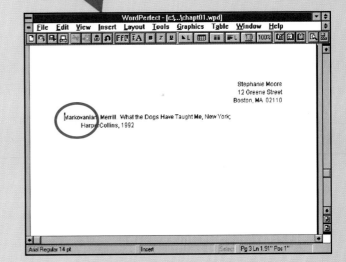

TASK 32
Creating a Bulleted List

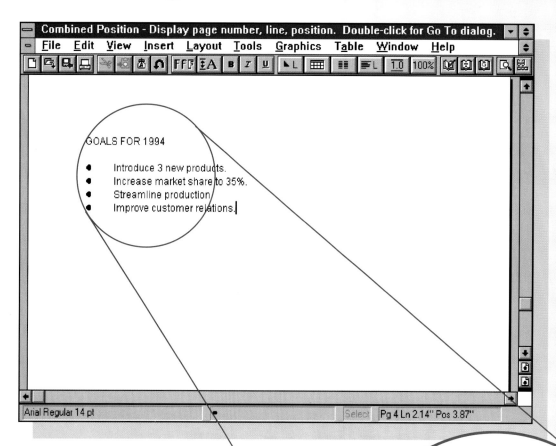

"Why would I do this?"

Bulleted lists are good when you want to present a series of ideas. A bulleted list helps the readers visually follow along. For example, you can create a bulleted list for goals, an agenda, an overhead slide, or a list of key points you want to cover at a meeting.

In your manuscript, move to the bottom of the document and create a new page.

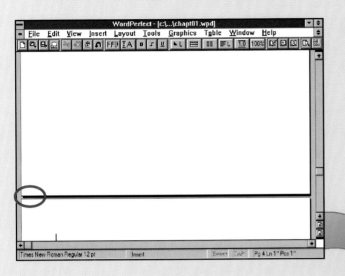

1 Press **Ctrl+End** or scroll to the bottom of the document. Then, press **Ctrl+Enter** to insert a page break.

2 On page 4, type the text that appears in the figure so that your computer screen matches the screen in the book.

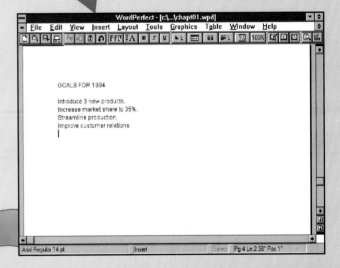

3 Select all the lines except for Goals for 1994, to include in the bulleted list. This step selects the text to which you want to add bullets.

Task 32: Creating a Bulleted List

4 Click **Insert** in the menu bar. Then, click **Bullets and Numbers**. You see the Bullets and Numbers dialog box.

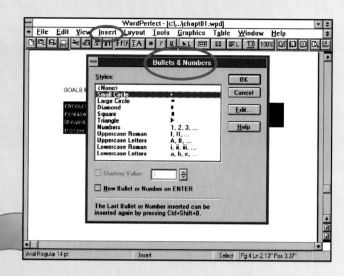

5 In the Styles list, click the large circle bullet. This selects the type of bullet that you want to insert. Click **OK** to insert the bullets.

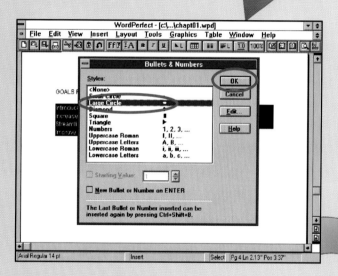

6 The text is indented. Next, click outside the selected text to deselect it. Now you can see the bulleted list better.

WHY WORRY?

To remove the bullets in the list, immediately click the Undo button in the Power Bar. Or delete the bullets as you would any other character: use the Backspace or Del key.

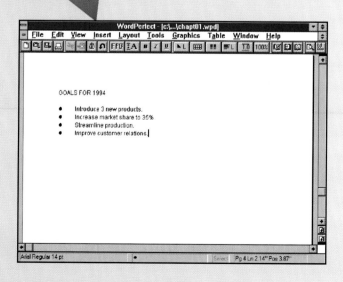

Creating a Numbered List

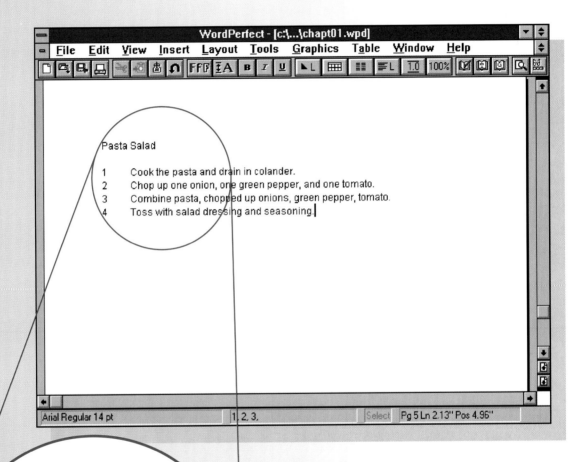

"Why would I do this?"

Numbered lists are good when you want to present a series of ideas. A numbered list helps the readers visually follow along. For example, you can create a numbered list for a set of instructions, a recipe, or a list of key points you want to cover at a meeting.

In your manuscript, move to the bottom of the document and create a new page. Then, type a list containing five items, and add numbers to the items in the list.

Task 33: Creating a Numbered List

1 Press **Ctrl+End** or scroll to the bottom of the document. Then, press **Ctrl+Enter** to insert a page break.

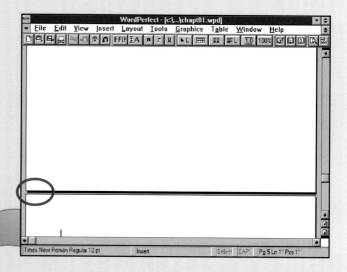

2 On page 5, type the text that appears in the figure so that your computer screen matches the screen in the book.

3 Select all the lines, except the Pasta Salad line, to include in the numbered list. This step selects the text to which you want to add numbers.

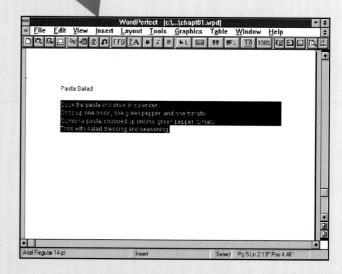

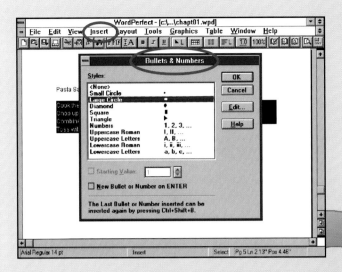

4 Click **Insert** in the menu bar. Then, click **Bullets and Numbers**. This selects the Insert Bullets and Numbers command. You see the Bullets and Numbers dialog box.

5 In the Styles list, click **Numbers**. This selects the Numbers option. Click **OK**.

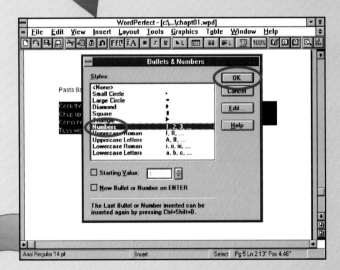

6 This inserts the numbers and indents the text. Next, click outside the selected text to deselect it. Now you can see the numbered list better.

WHY WORRY?

To remove the numbers in the list, immediately click the Undo button on the Power Bar. Or delete the numbers as you would any other character: use the Backspace or Del key.

Setting Tabs

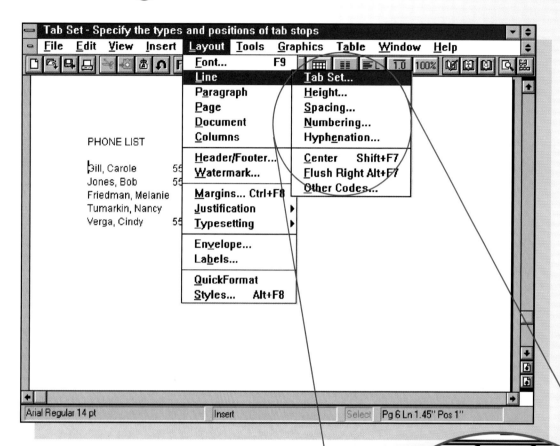

"Why would I do this?"

You can set different types of tab stops—left (default), right, decimal, or center tabs. You also can insert a dot leader before a tab stop. Setting a default tab is useful for creating a table that contains one or more columns.

First let's type the text for a two-column table. Then we will set a left tab for the second column at three inches from the left margin.

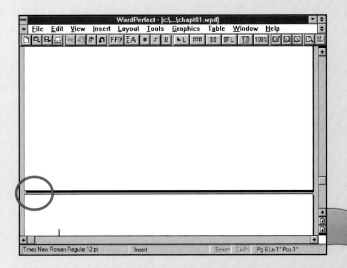

1 Press **Ctrl+End** or scroll to the bottom of the document. Then, press **Ctrl+Enter** to insert a page break.

2 On page 6, type the text that appears in the figure so that your computer screen matches the screen in the book. Be sure to press Tab after typing each name in the list.

NOTE ▼

WordPerfect applies the same settings to every paragraph until it encounters a change. The tab settings are placed at the beginning of the paragraph you are in when you make the changes. These changes affect all text that follows until you change the tab settings again.

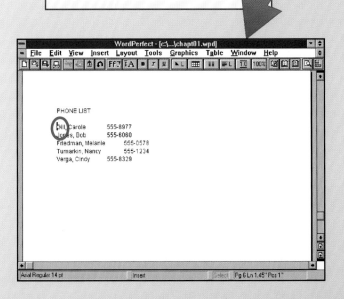

3 Click before the G in *Gill*. This moves the insertion point to the top of the list to ensure that tab changes affect the entire list.

Task 34: Setting Tabs

4 Click **Layout** in the menu bar. Then, click **Line**.

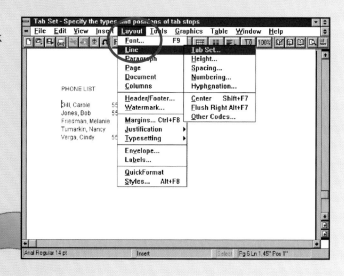

5 Click **Tab Set** to select the Tab Set command. You see the Tab Set dialog box.

6 Click **Clear All**. This step selects the Clear All button. All the tabs are cleared so that you can set new tabs.

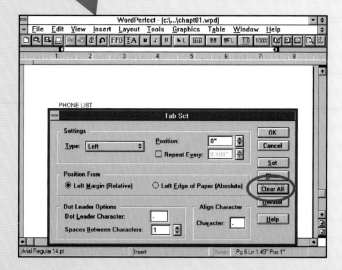

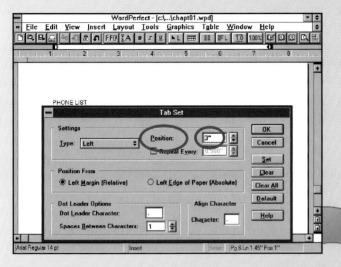

7 Double-click in the **Position** text box and type **3**. This step highlights the position number in the box and specifies the tab at three inches from the left margin.

NOTE ▼

You can choose different types of tab stops—left (default), right, decimal, and center tabs.

8 Click **Set**. This step confirms the new tab setting. Click **OK**.

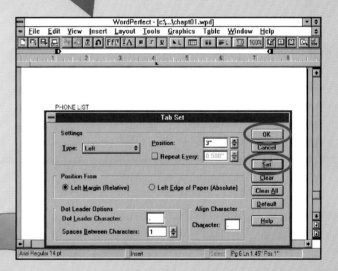

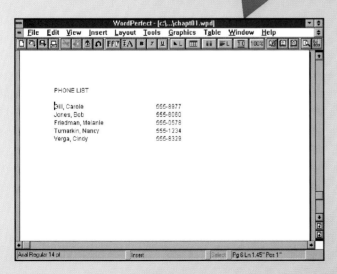

9 This step closes the dialog box. The default tab is three inches from the left margin.

WHY WORRY?

To revert to the default tab settings, display the Reveal Codes (press Alt+F3) and delete the Tab Set code.

Double-Spacing a Document

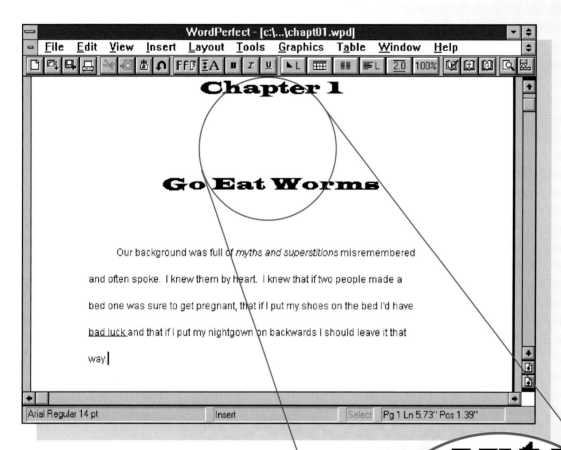

"Why would I do this?"

WordPerfect for Windows enables you to adjust line spacing to improve the appearance of a document. The most common line-spacing options include single-spacing (default), 1 1/2 lines, and double-spacing. For example, you might want to double-space a draft, a manuscript, or a script, so you can mark your changes more easily on the printed pages.

In your manuscript, let's double-space the text on page 1.

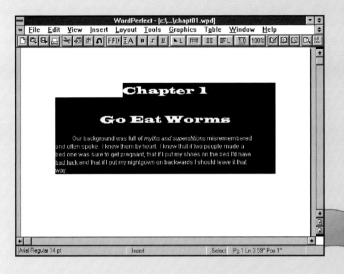

1 Press **Ctrl+Home** to move to the top of the document. Then, hold down the mouse button and drag the mouse to select all the text on page 1. This step selects the text you want to double-space.

2 Click the **Line Spacing** button (the button that contains the number 1.0) on the Power Bar, hold down the mouse button, and drag to the **2.0** option. Then, release the mouse button. This step tells WordPerfect to double-space the selected text.

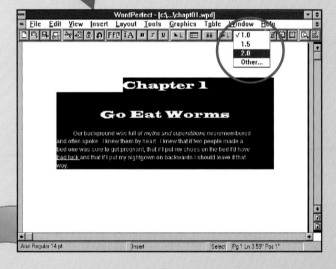

3 Click outside the selected text to deselect the text.

WHY WORRY?

To undo the line spacing change, click the Undo button on the Power Bar immediately.

TASK 36

Displaying WordPerfect Codes

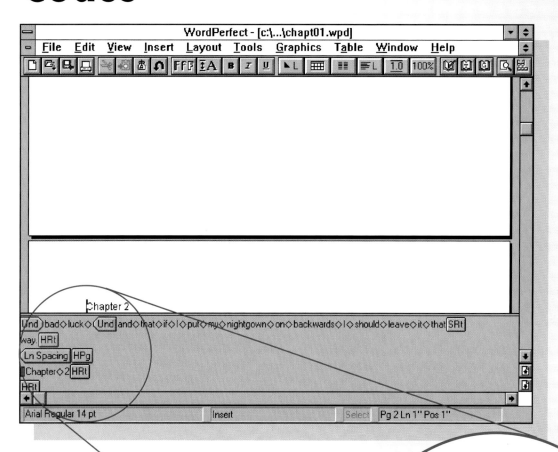

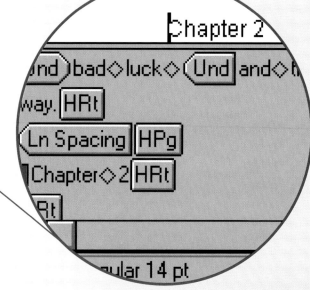

"Why would I do this?"

Every time you make a formatting change to your document, WordPerfect inserts a code in the Reveal Codes window but not on the editing screen. The codes tell WordPerfect when to use tabs, margin settings, hard returns, and so on. For example, a hard return in your document displays as HRt in the Reveal Codes window. You can delete codes in the Reveal Codes window to remove formatting in your document.

Let's display WordPerfect's Reveal Codes window.

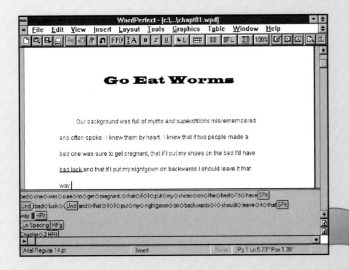

1 Press **Alt+F3**. Pressing Alt+F3 selects the View Reveal Codes command. The insertion point can be anywhere in the text when you select the command. The screen is divided horizontally, and the text appears in both windows. The lower part of the screen shows the hidden codes.

NOTE ▼

Make the Reveal Codes area larger or smaller by placing the mouse pointer on the line separating the windows. Drag the bar up or down.

2 Press → three times. This step moves the insertion in sync in both windows. The insertion point in the Reveal Codes window is a red rectangular block.

WHY WORRY?

To return the screen to normal display, press Alt+F3 again.

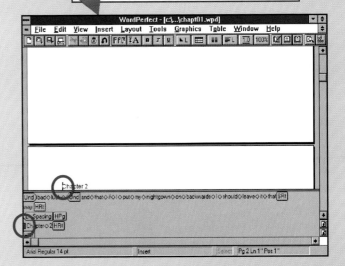

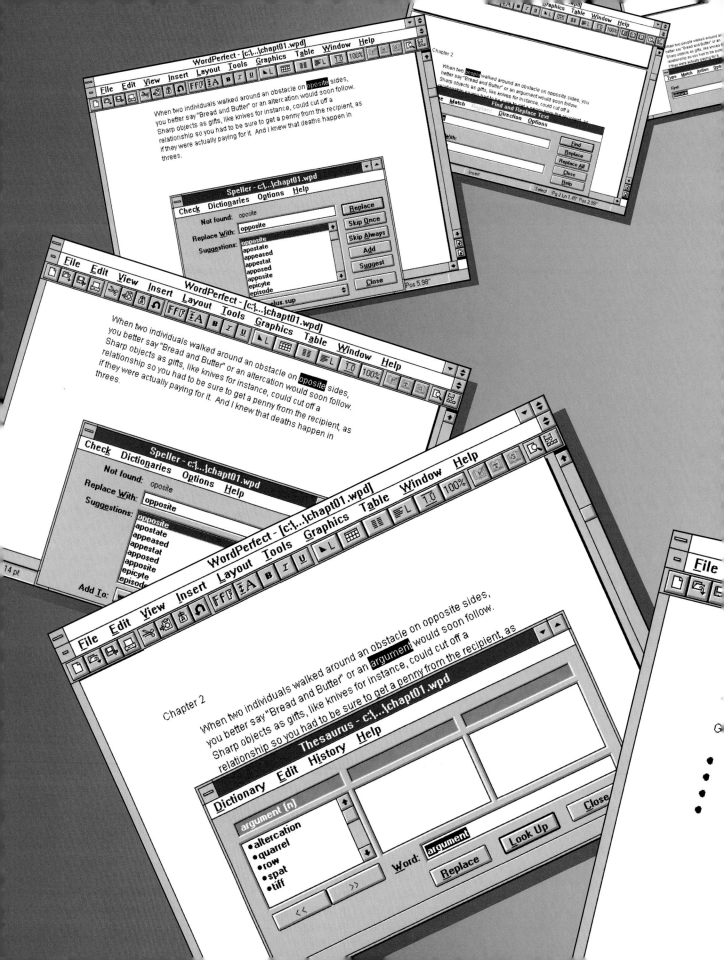

PART V
More Editing

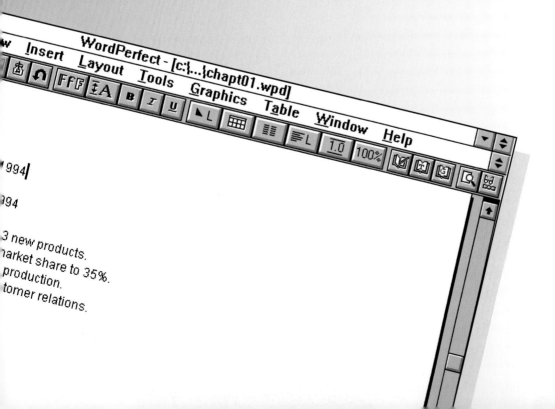

This part shows you how to search for text, find and replace text, check your spelling, look up a word in the thesaurus, check your grammar, insert the date, and insert a special character.

The *Find* command enables you to locate specific text in your document. You can indicate the direction (forward or backward), specify case-sensitive for an exact match, search for whole words only (to prevent finding text that is part of another word), and include headers and footers in your search.

WordPerfect's *Find and Replace* feature lets you change a word, a phrase, or codes throughout the document quickly and easily. The Find and Replace command gives you several search options to hone the search. The Type option lets you specify the type of information you want to find, such as text or specific codes.

The *Match Whole Word* option lets you search for text with the specified combination of upper- and lowercase letters. The Match Whole Word option searches for whole words only, and does not find occurrences of the word that are part of other words. The *Match Font* option lets you search for a specific font in your document. The *Match Codes* option lets you search for a code, such as the Bold code.

The *Direction Forward* option searches forward, and the *Direction Backward* option searches backward.

With the *Spelling* feature, you can create supplemental dictionaries for medical, legal, and technical documents to ensure accuracy when spell-checking special terms for documents in those fields.

WordPerfect's electronic Thesaurus helps you improve the language in your document. There are three types of words that appear in the Thesaurus dialog box: *headwords*, *references*, and *subgroups*. The word you look up is called the headword. The headword appears at the top of the column. The part of speech enclosed in parentheses appears next to the word you are looking up. For example, (n) indicates a noun and (v) indicates a verb.

References are synonyms and antonyms marked with a bullet; you can look up any of these words for more ideas. Subgroups are groups of words with the same basic meaning that appear below headwords.

WordPerfect provides another proofreading tool called *Grammatik*, a grammar checker which checks your document for correct grammar and use of language. You can specify grammar rule and writing style options to customize the grammar checker to meet your specific needs.

The Date feature enables you to enter the current date in your document. In this part, you learn how to insert date text. The default format for dates is Month, Day, Year; for instance, October 6, 1994. You also can change the date format with the Date Format command.

Instead of inserting the date text, you can insert a date code into your document. Each time you retrieve the document, the date will be updated to the current date. To do this, select the *Insert Date Date Code* command.

You can include special characters in your document, such as symbols, Greek letters, and scientific symbols. *Iconic symbols* are decorative characters such as bullets, stars, and flowers. You can choose the Multinational character set to insert foreign language characters such as tildes (~) and umlauts (¨).

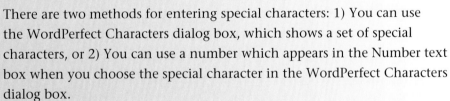

There are two methods for entering special characters: 1) You can use the WordPerfect Characters dialog box, which shows a set of special characters, or 2) You can use a number which appears in the Number text box when you choose the special character in the WordPerfect Characters dialog box.

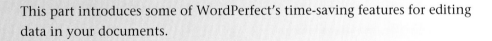

This part introduces some of WordPerfect's time-saving features for editing data in your documents.

Searching for Text

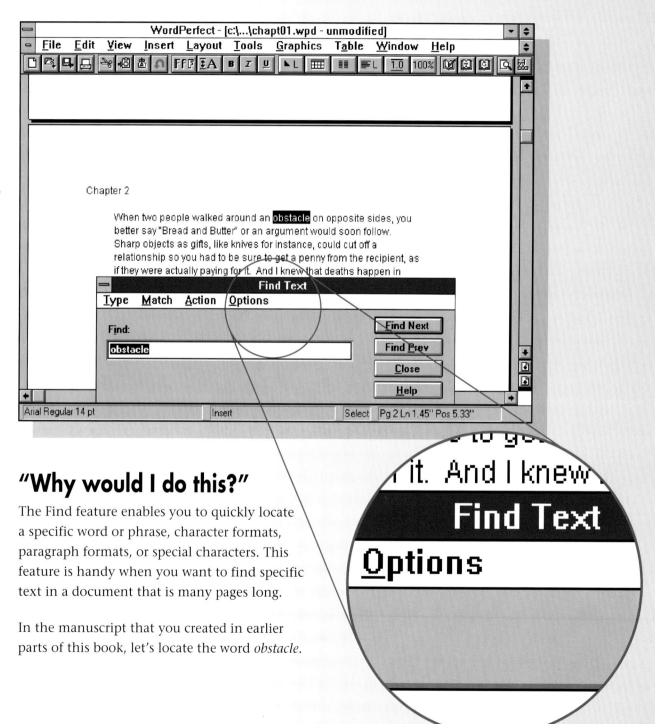

"Why would I do this?"

The Find feature enables you to quickly locate a specific word or phrase, character formats, paragraph formats, or special characters. This feature is handy when you want to find specific text in a document that is many pages long.

In the manuscript that you created in earlier parts of this book, let's locate the word *obstacle*.

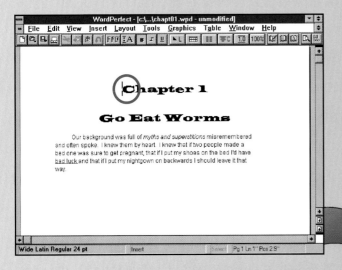

1 Press **Ctrl+Home**. This step moves the insertion point to the beginning of the document. When you begin the search, WordPerfect searches from the location of the insertion point forward, unless you tell WordPerfect to search backwards.

2 Press **F2**. Pressing F2 selects the Edit Find command. You see the Find Text dialog box. The insertion point is in the Find text box.

> **NOTE** ▼
>
> The Find Text dialog box includes the Find text box and other menu options that control how the program searches the document. (See your WordPerfect for Windows documentation for complete information on all the options.)

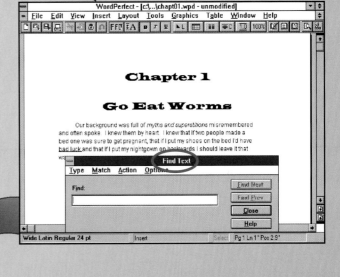

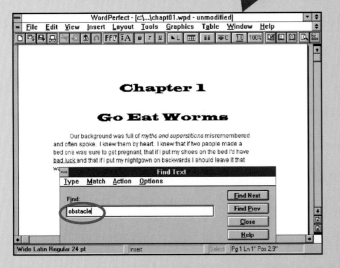

3 Type **obstacle**. This text, called the *search string*, is what you want to find.

> **NOTE** ▼
>
> By default, WordPerfect finds any occurrence of this text whether the letters are upper- or lowercase. You can specify that you want to find only whole words and to match case. To do so, click Match in the menu bar of the Find Text dialog box. Then click on Whole Word or Case.

Task 37: Searching for Text

4 Click **Find Next**. This starts the search. WordPerfect finds the first occurrence of the search string and selects that text. The dialog box remains open on-screen. Click **Close**.

NOTE ▼

To search for the next occurrence of the search string, select the Find Next button again. To search backwards to find the previous occurrence, click Find Prev.

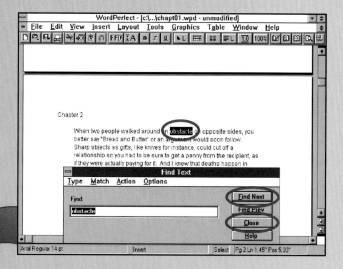

5 This step closes the dialog box.

NOTE ▼

If you want to repeat the search after you have closed the Find Text dialog box, press Shift+F2 to repeat the search.

WHY WORRY?

If WordPerfect doesn't find the text, you see an alert message. Click OK and try the search again. Double-check that you typed the search string correctly. Also, be sure that the insertion point is at the top of the document.

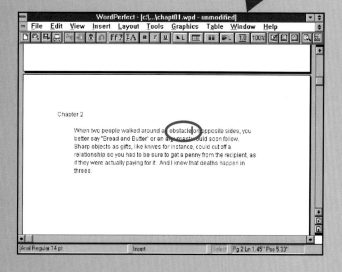

TASK 38

Finding and Replacing Text

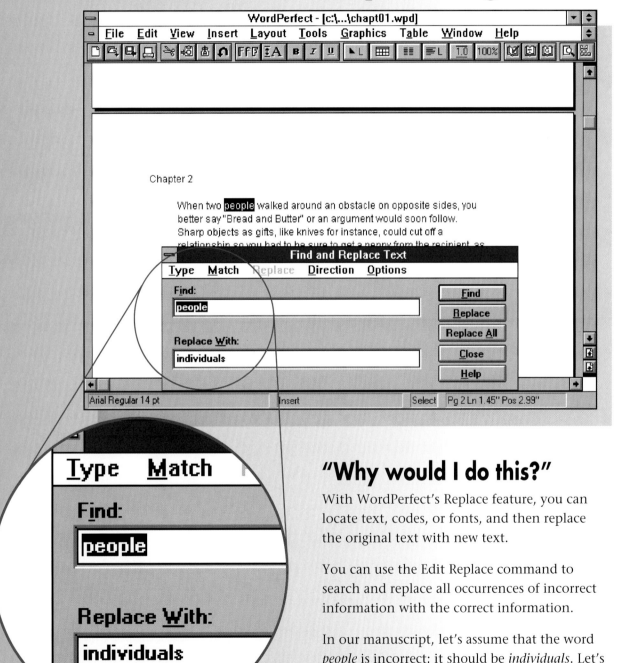

"Why would I do this?"

With WordPerfect's Replace feature, you can locate text, codes, or fonts, and then replace the original text with new text.

You can use the Edit Replace command to search and replace all occurrences of incorrect information with the correct information.

In our manuscript, let's assume that the word *people* is incorrect; it should be *individuals*. Let's replace all occurrences of *people* with *individuals*.

Task 38: Finding and Replacing Text

1 Press **Ctrl+Home**. This moves the insertion point to the beginning of the document. When you begin the search, WordPerfect searches from the location of the insertion point forward, unless you tell WordPerfect to search backwards.

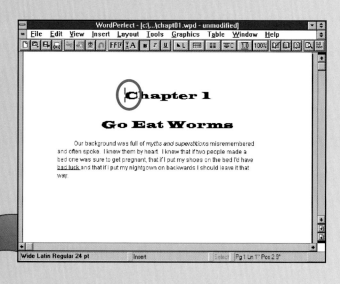

2 Press **Ctrl+F2**. Pressing Ctrl+F2 selects the Edit Replace command. WordPerfect displays the Find and Replace Text dialog box. The insertion point is in the Find text box. Notice that the previous search string appears in the Find box.

3 Type **people** and press **Tab**. This text, called the *search string*, is what you want to find. Pressing Tab moves the insertion point to the Replace With text box.

NOTE ▼

The Replace dialog box includes the Find text box, the Replace With text box, and other menu options that control how the program performs the search and replace operation.

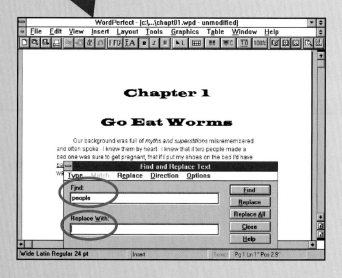

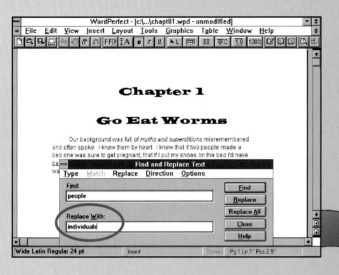

4 Type **individuals**. This is the text you want to use as the replacement.

5 Click **Find.** This starts the search. WordPerfect finds the first occurrence of the search string and selects that text. The dialog box remains open on-screen.

> **NOTE** ▼
>
> If you need to see the text hidden by the dialog box, you can move the dialog box out of the way by pointing to the title bar at the top of the dialog box, holding down the mouse button, and dragging the dialog box by its title bar to the new location.

6 Click **Replace.** This selects the Replace button. WordPerfect replaces the selected text with the next text and then moves to the next occurrence of the search string. The dialog box remains open on-screen.

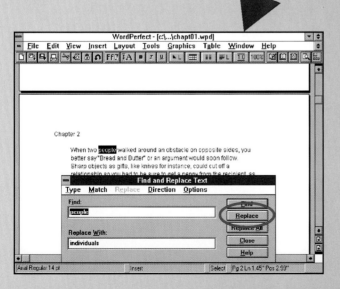

Task 38: Finding and Replacing Text

7 Click **Replace** again. WordPerfect replaces the selected occurrence of the text and then moves to the next occurrence of the search string. When WordPerfect finds no more occurrences of the search string, you see an alert box.

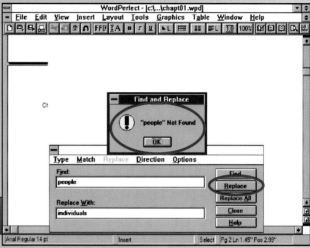

> **NOTE** ▼
>
> To replace all occurrences of the text automatically, click on the Replace All button. However, test the search and replace strings by doing a single replacement first.

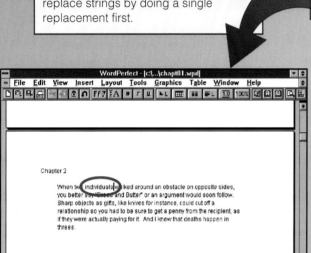

8 Click **OK.** This closes the alert box. The dialog box remains open. Click **Close** to close the dialog box. Now you can see the replaced text.

> **WHY WORRY?**
>
> Be careful about making replacements that might not have occurred to you, such as replacing all occurrences of "and" with "or" only to end up with words like "sor" and "Rory."

Checking Your Spelling

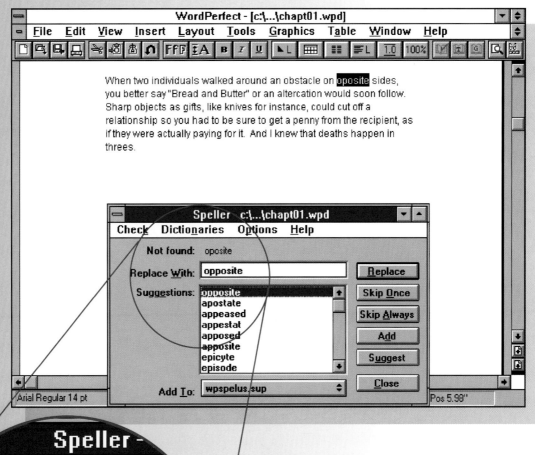

"Why would I do this?"

WordPerfect's spell checker rapidly finds and highlights for correction the misspellings in a document. Spell checking is an important feature that makes your documents look professional and letter-perfect.

If there are any misspelled words in your manuscript, WordPerfect will find them. However, just to make sure that WordPerfect finds some spelling errors, let's make an intentional typo.

Task 39: Checking Your Spelling

1 On page 2 in the document, in the first sentence, remove the first occurrence of the letter *p* in the word *opposite*.

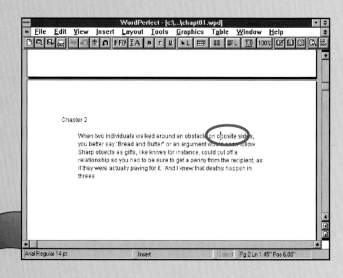

2 To begin the spell checker, click the **Speller** button in the Power Bar (the button with the open book and a check mark). Clicking the Speller button selects the Speller command. You see the Speller dialog box. Click **Start**. This starts the spelling check.

> **NOTE** ▼
>
> You also can press Ctrl+F1 to select the Speller command.

3 WordPerfect finds and highlights for correction the word *misremembered* and displays the Speller dialog box. This word appears in the Not Found area at the top of the Speller dialog box. Even though the spell checker did not find the word *misremembered* in its dictionary, let's leave this word in our manuscript anyway. Click **Skip Always**.

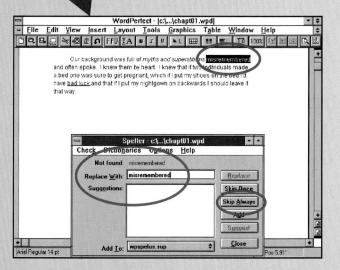

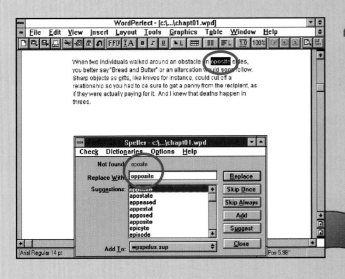

4 This option tells WordPerfect to skip all occurrences of this word. The spell checker finds the next misspelled word—*oposite*—and displays the word at the top of the Speller dialog box. Click **Replace**. This replaces the incorrect word with the correct word in the document. Next, correct the rest of the words in the document.

WHY WORRY?

To stop the spell check, click Close after WordPerfect stops on a word.

5 When the spell checker doesn't find any more misspelled words, the program displays a dialog box containing the message: `Spell-check completed. Close Speller?` Click **Yes**.

NOTE ▼

You can click the Add button to add words to WordPerfect's dictionary.

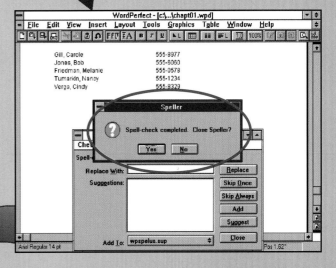

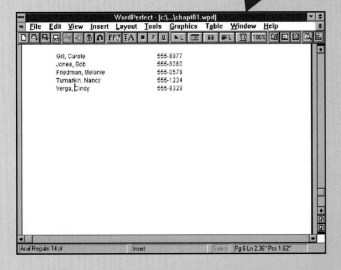

6 The dialog box closes and the spell check is complete.

TASK 40

Looking Up a Word in the Thesaurus

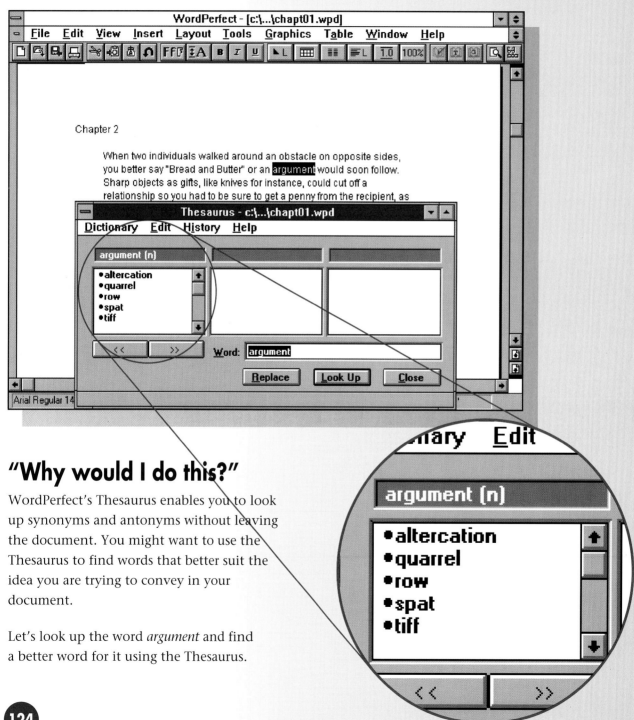

"Why would I do this?"

WordPerfect's Thesaurus enables you to look up synonyms and antonyms without leaving the document. You might want to use the Thesaurus to find words that better suit the idea you are trying to convey in your document.

Let's look up the word *argument* and find a better word for it using the Thesaurus.

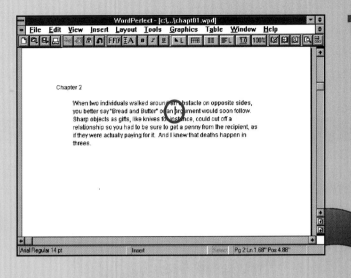

1 On page 2, click before the word *argument* in the first sentence. Argument is the word that you want to look up in the Thesaurus. You can click before the word or within the word you want to look up.

NOTE ▼

You also can select the specific word you want to look up.

2 Click the **Thesaurus** button in the Power Bar (the button with the open book and the letter T). The Word text box at the bottom of the dialog box displays the selected word. WordPerfect displays a list of synonyms for the selected word. Click **altercation**. Then, click **Replace**.

NOTE ▼

You also can press Alt+F1 to select the Thesaurus command.

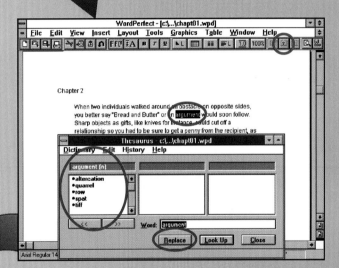

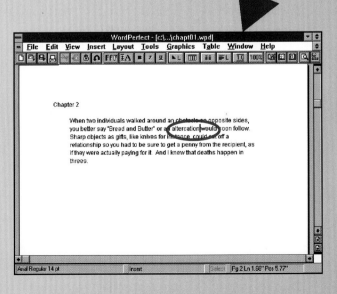

3 WordPerfect replaces the original word (argument) with the new word (altercation), and closes the dialog box.

WHY WORRY?

To undo the replacement, click the Undo button in the Power Bar immediately.

TASK 41

Checking Your Grammar

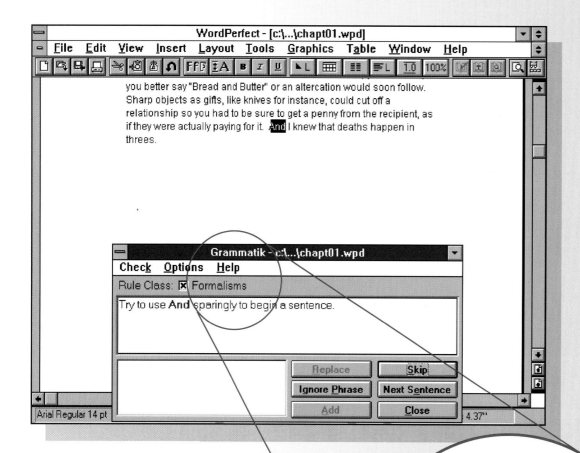

"Why would I do this?"

WordPerfect's grammar checker (called Grammatik) examines each sentence in your document and determines whether the text conforms to various grammar, style, usage, and punctuation rules.

If there are any grammar, style, usage, or punctuation errors in your manuscript, WordPerfect will find them. Let's run the grammar checker and correct the errors now.

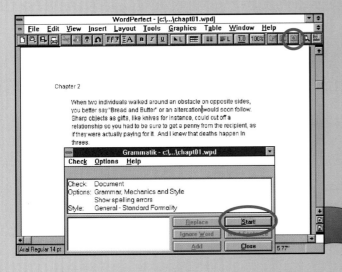

1 Click the **Grammatik** button in the Power Bar (the button with the open book and the letter G). You see the Grammatik dialog box. This dialog box enables you to control how the grammar check is performed. For this task, the default settings are appropriate. Click **Start**. This starts the grammar check.

NOTE ▼

You also can press Alt+Shift+F1 to select the Grammatik command.

2 WordPerfect finds the first error in a sentence and displays the Grammatik dialog box. This spelling error in the sentence is highlighted in the document. You see the Rule Class with an explanation of the grammar rule. The advice with an explanation on how to fix the error appears beneath the Rule Class. Click **Skip**. This skips the current suggestion and checks the next sentence.

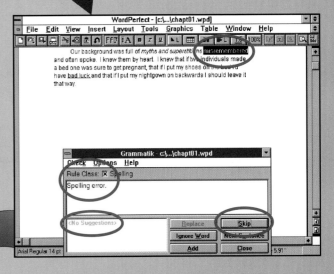

3 The grammar checker finds the next error and suggests that you replace the word *that* with the word *which*. Click **Replace**. This changes the sentence with the suggestion in the replacement area.

4 The grammar checker finds the next error and suggests that you revise the long sentence. Click **Skip**. This skips the current suggestion and checks the next sentence.

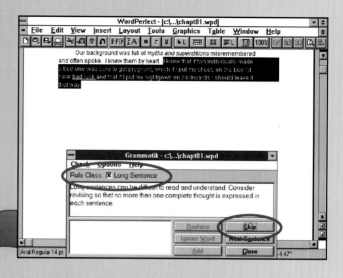

5 The grammar checker finds the next error and suggests that you use *And* sparingly to begin a sentence.

WHY WORRY?

To stop the grammar check, click Close after WordPerfect stops on a sentence.

6 Correct the rest of the grammar in the document. When the grammar checker doesn't find any more grammar errors, the program displays the following prompt: `Grammar check completed. Close Grammatik?` Click **Yes**. This closes the Grammatik dialog box.

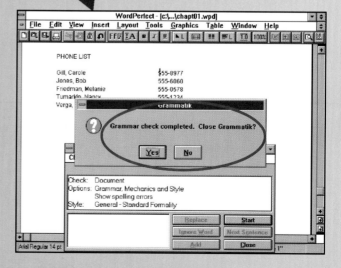

Inserting the Date

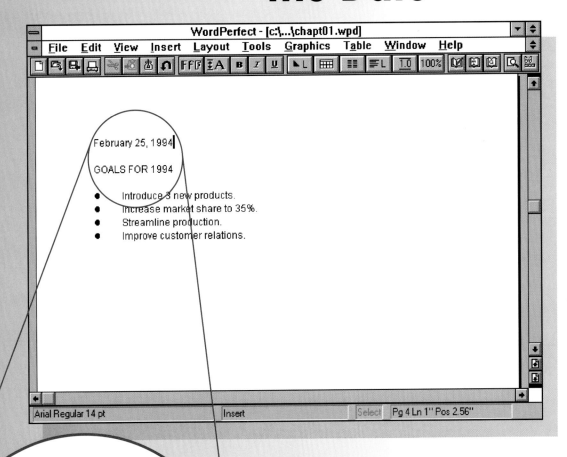

"Why would I do this?"

The Date command inserts the date or time into a document automatically. The date and time is received from the computer's clock. WordPerfect inserts the date when you print the document. You might want to insert the date into a letter or memo automatically instead of typing the date. Dates in a document also can help you keep track of the last time you modified your document.

In our manuscript document, let's insert the date.

Task 42: Inserting the Date

1 Click at the top of page 3. This places the insertion point where you want the date to appear.

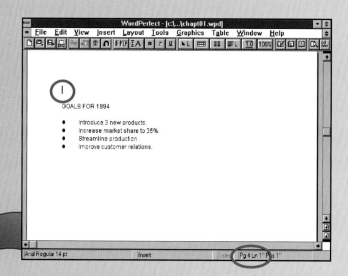

2 Click **Insert** in the menu bar. Then, click **Date**. This selects the Insert Date command. You see a list of Date options. Click **Date Text**. This selects the Date Text command.

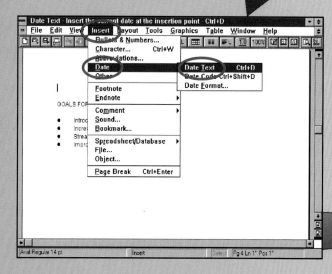

3 The current date is inserted into your document, and the insertion point is placed after the date text. The date that is inserted into your document will differ from the one in the figure.

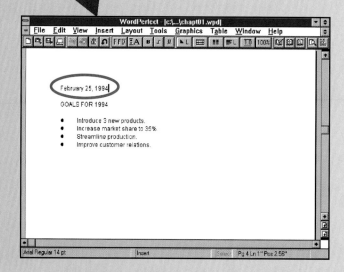

Inserting a Special Character

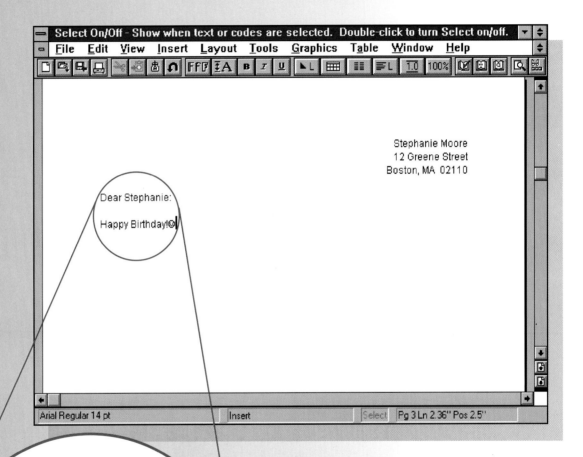

"Why would I do this?"

You can insert many special characters into your document. The WordPerfect Characters dialog box gives you access to symbols and other special characters. Perhaps you want to insert a copyright symbol, a registered trademark symbol, or a foreign language symbol in your document.

Let's add some text to your letter on page 3. Then we will insert a smiley face symbol.

Task 43: Inserting a Special Character

1 Click below the address on page 3 and press Ctrl+Enter to insert a page break. Then, scroll up to page 3. Next, type **Dear Stephanie:**, press **Enter** twice, and type **Happy Birthday!**. This enters additional text in the letter.

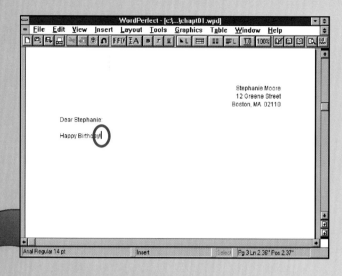

2 Click **Insert** in the menu bar. This opens the Insert menu and displays the Insert commands. Click **Character**. This selects the Character command.

3 You see the WordPerfect Characters dialog box. This box lists the selected set, displays the characters within that set, and lists the number of the selected character. The selected set is Iconic Symbols. The first character, a heart, is selected.

NOTE ▼

You also can press Ctrl+W to select the Insert Character command.

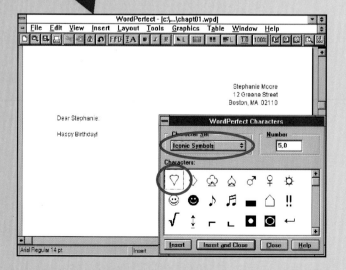

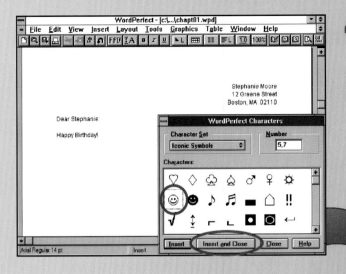

4 Click on the smiley face. This selects the symbol you want to insert. Click the **Insert and Close** button.

5 WordPerfect inserts the symbol and closes the dialog box.

WHY WORRY?

To undo the insertion, click the Undo button in the Power Bar or delete the character; press Backspace or Delete.

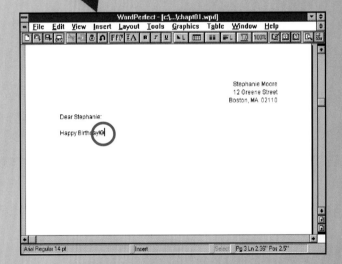

PART VI

More Formatting

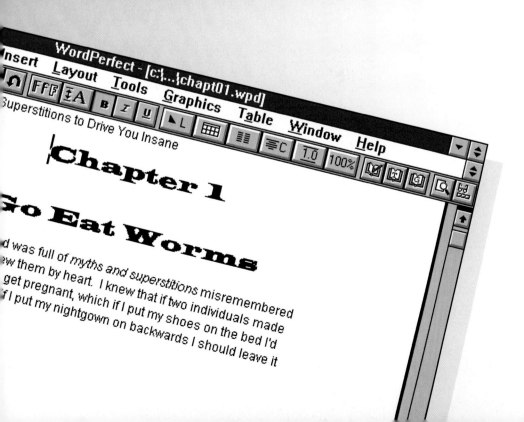

Part VI: More Formatting

In this part, you learn how to add a border to a paragraph, shade a paragraph, set margins, number pages, and create and edit headers and footers.

One of the best ways to enhance the appearance of a document is to add borders to the text. You can use the Paragraph Border/Fill command to add boxes around paragraphs and shade paragraphs. You can even customize the appearance of the border. You can, for example, create a box with a line as thin as a hairline or a thick line.

You can use a border to bring attention to an important paragraph on a page, improve the page design by creating a border around an entire page, or separate text columns in a bulletin or newsletter.

The percentage of shading as a background can be between 0 and 100. A 10 to 25 percent shaded background works best. Adding a border and shading works for document headings or sections of a document that you want to set off. The Sample Documents section (Part X) contains several documents that show off these features.

WordPerfect measures left and right margins from the right and left edges of the paper or from the perforation for pin-feed paper. Changing the margins allows you to set the horizontal and vertical position of the text on the printed page. The default left, right, top, and bottom margins are set to one inch. You can change any of the margin settings in the Margins dialog box.

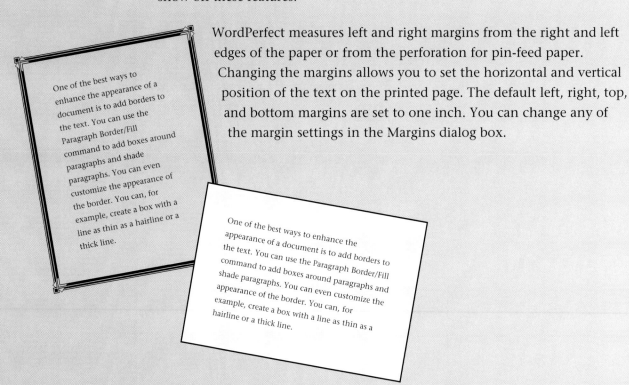

One of the best ways to enhance the appearance of a document is to add borders to the text. You can use the Paragraph Border/Fill command to add boxes around paragraphs and shade paragraphs. You can even customize the appearance of the border. You can, for example, create a box with a line as thin as a hairline or a thick line.

One of the best ways to enhance the appearance of a document is to add borders to the text. You can use the Paragraph Border/Fill command to add boxes around paragraphs and shade paragraphs. You can even customize the appearance of the border. You can, for example, create a box with a line as thin as a hairline or a thick line.

137

When you add page numbers with the Page Numbering command, you can specify whether to add the page numbers to the top of each page (to a header) or to the bottom of each page (to a footer). You also can specify the alignment: left, center, or right.

WordPerfect lets you add headers and footers to print information at the top and bottom of every page of the printout. You can create your own header and footer information such as chapter headings, dates, or page numbers. Also, you can include any text and boldface, italicize, or center the text to control the appearance of the header or footer.

After you create a header or footer, you can edit the header or footer information easily. You can insert, delete, copy, and move text within a header or footer as you can any text in a document. If you no longer want the header or footer, you even can delete all the text to remove the header or footer altogether.

This part shows you formatting operations you need for enhancing the appearance and layout of your documents.

The percentage of shading as a background can be between 0 and 100. A 10 to 25 percent shaded background works best. Adding a border and shading works for document headings or sections of a document that you want to set off. The Sample Documents section (Part X) contains several documents that show off these features.

Adding a Paragraph Border

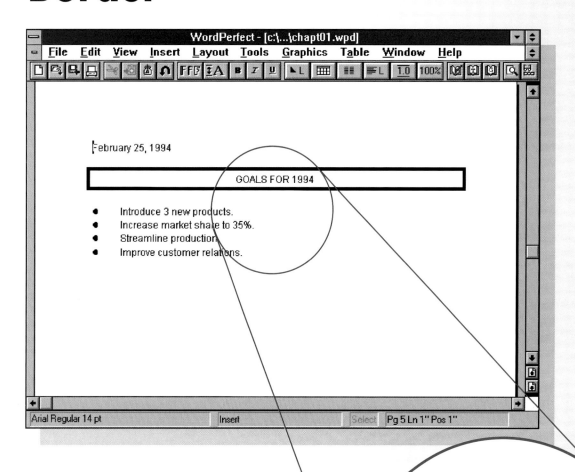

"Why would I do this?"

WordPerfect's Border/Fill command lets you add boxes around paragraphs with a single line. You can, for example, have a single thick outline border that creates a box to emphasize the title for the document.

In your manuscript document, add a box around the title on page 5 to draw attention to it.

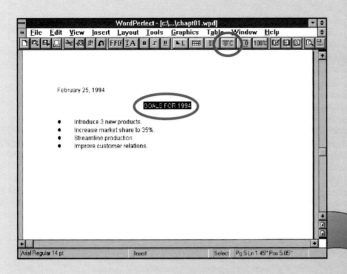

1 Scroll to page 5. Select the title *Goals for 1994*. Click **Justification** in the Power Bar, and choose **Center** to center the text. Leave the text selected so that you can add a border.

2 Click **Layout** in the menu bar; then click **Paragraph**. This selects the Layout Paragraph command and displays a submenu. Click **Border/Fill** from the submenu. This selects the Border/Fill command.

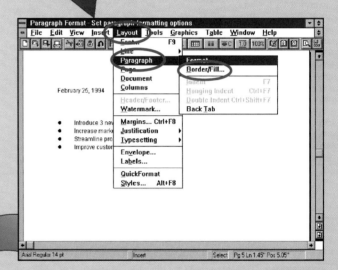

3 You see the Paragraph Border dialog box. You can select the type of border you want from this dialog box.

Task 44: Adding a Paragraph Border

4 Click the pull-down button in the **Border Style** list. A list of border styles appear. Then, click **Thick** in the Border Style list. This tells WordPerfect what border style you want for the border. Click **OK**. This confirms the change and returns you to the document.

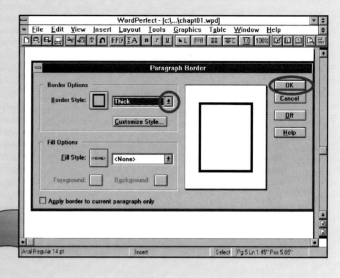

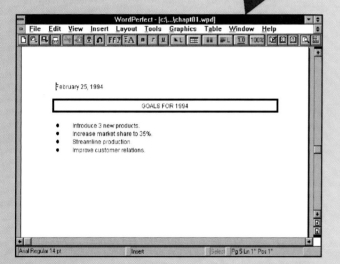

5 The paragraph now has a border. Click outside the text to deselect it.

WHY WORRY?

To remove the border, immediately click the Undo button on the Power Bar. If you don't undo the change immediately, you have to use a different method. To do so, display Reveal codes (press Alt+F3); then delete the Para Border code.

Shading a Paragraph

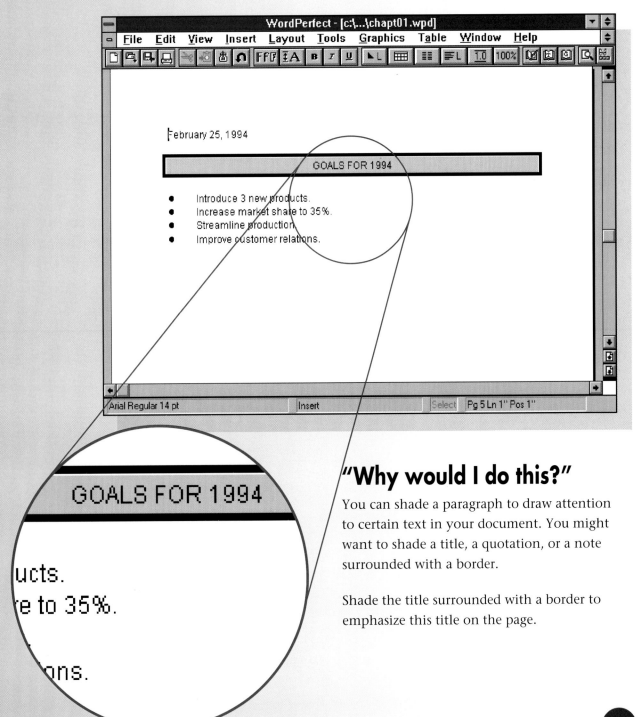

"Why would I do this?"

You can shade a paragraph to draw attention to certain text in your document. You might want to shade a title, a quotation, or a note surrounded with a border.

Shade the title surrounded with a border to emphasize this title on the page.

Task 45: Shading a Paragraph

1 Select the title *Goals for 1994*. This is the paragraph you want to shade.

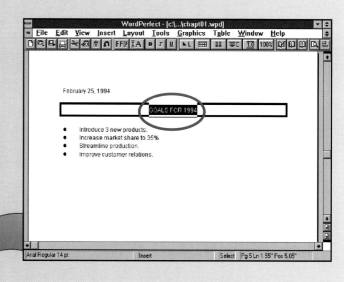

2 Click **Layout** in the menu bar; then click **Paragraph**. This selects the Layout Paragraph command and displays a submenu. Click **Border/Fill**. This selects the Border/Fill command.

3 You see the Paragraph Border dialog box. You can select the type of fill you want from this dialog box.

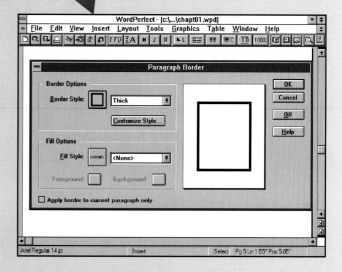

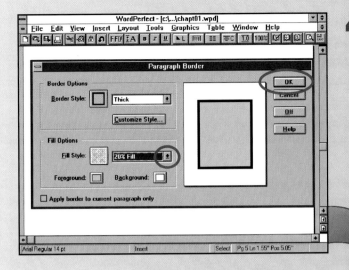

4 Click the pull-down button in the **Fill Style** list. A list of fill styles appears. Click **20% Fill** in the Fill Style list. This tells WordPerfect what fill style you want for the fill. Click **OK**. This confirms the change and returns you to the document.

5 The paragraph now has a fill. Click outside the selected text. This deselects the text so you can see the shading better.

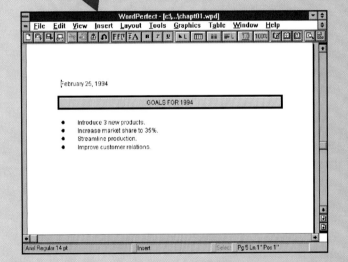

NOTE ▼

Depending on your printer, the shading might print differently than it appears on-screen.

WHY WORRY?

To remove the shading, immediately click the Undo button on the Power Bar. Alternatively, you can display Reveal codes (press Alt+F3) and then delete the Para Border code.

Setting Margins

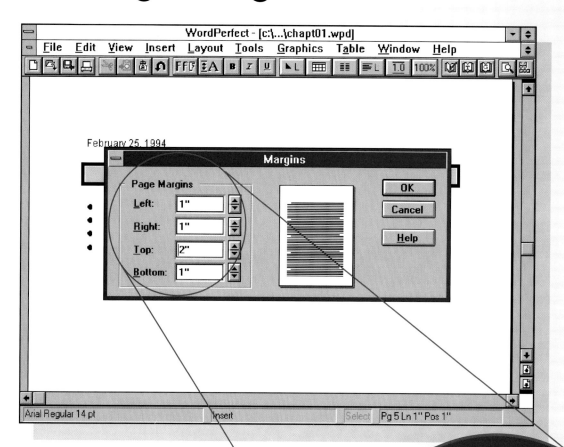

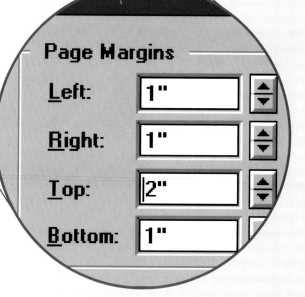

"Why would I do this?"

You can adjust the left, right, top, and bottom margins. You might want to change the margin settings for either the entire document or for the document pages from the current position of the insertion point. Margins also can be changed for a single paragraph or a single page.

Let's set a two-inch top margin for the entire document.

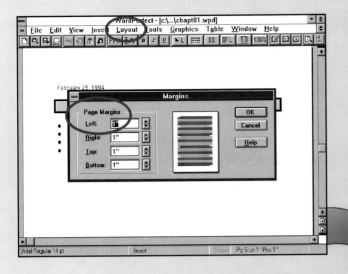

1 Click **Layout** in the menu bar; then, click **Margins**. This selects the Layout Margins command. You see the Margins dialog box. You see text boxes for each of the four margins: Left, Right, Top, and Bottom. The Left entry is selected.

NOTE ▼

You also can press Ctrl+F8 to select the Layout Margins command. The default for the left, right, top, and bottom margins is one inch.

2 Press Tab twice to move to the **Top** entry box. Next, type **2**. This specifies a 2-inch top margin. You see a sample of the margins on the right side of the dialog box. Click **OK**.

WHY WORRY?

To cancel the margin change, click Cancel in the Margins dialog box.

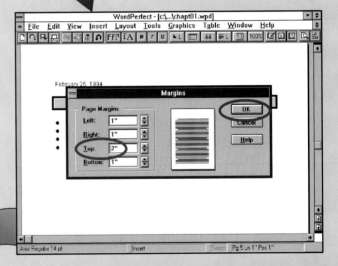

3 This confirms the new margin settings and closes the dialog box.

NOTE ▼

To see the effect of the margin changes, you must view the document in Full Page view.

TASK 47
Adding Page Numbers

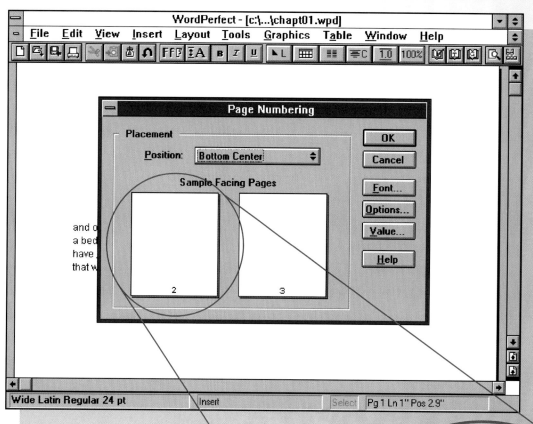

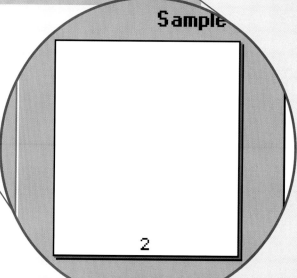

"Why would I do this?"

WordPerfect gives you a page numbering feature that automatically inserts page numbers and prints the page numbers in the position you specify. That way, you don't have to manually enter and manage the page numbers. Page numbering is often used on manuscript pages or reports.

Let's number the pages in the manuscript document.

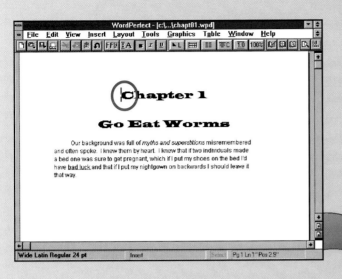

1 Press **Ctrl+Home**. This moves the insertion point to the top of the document to ensure that all pages will be numbered.

2 Click **Layout** in the menu bar. Then, click **Page**. This selects the Layout Page command and displays a menu of Page options. Click **Numbering**. This selects the Numbering command.

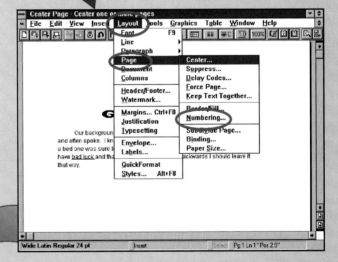

3 The Page Numbering dialog box appears. You can use this box to specify many options—position, numbering options, and so on.

4 Click the drop-down arrow in the **Position** list, and drag the mouse down to highlight **Bottom Center**. This displays a list of position options and selects Bottom Center. This option tells WordPerfect to insert page numbers at the bottom center of every page. Click **OK**. This confirms the page numbering settings, closes the dialog box, and returns you to the document.

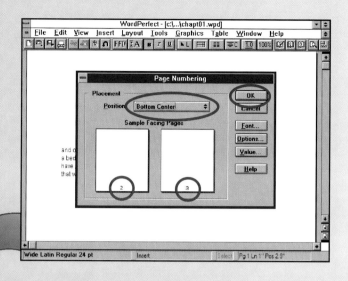

5 On-screen, you cannot see the page numbers. To do so, you must view the document in Full Page view.

6 To view the document, click **View** on the menu bar, click **Zoom**, and choose **Full Page**. To return to 100% view, click **View** in the menu bar, click **Zoom**, and choose **100%**.

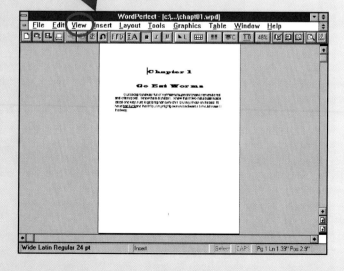

Creating a Header or Footer

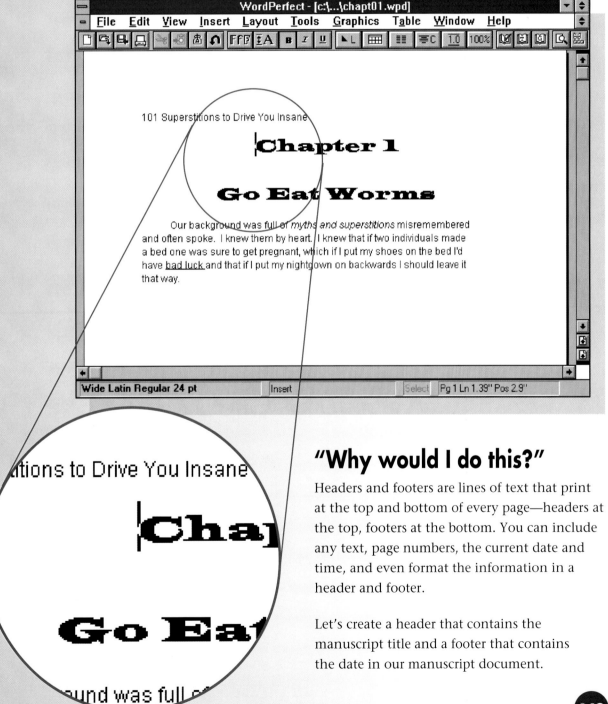

"Why would I do this?"

Headers and footers are lines of text that print at the top and bottom of every page—headers at the top, footers at the bottom. You can include any text, page numbers, the current date and time, and even format the information in a header and footer.

Let's create a header that contains the manuscript title and a footer that contains the date in our manuscript document.

Task 48: Creating a Header or Footer

1 Press **Ctrl+Home**. This moves the insertion point to the top of the document to ensure that the new header will be inserted on every page of the document.

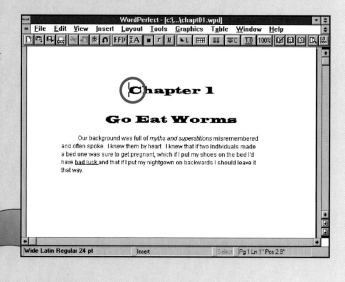

2 Click **Layout** in the menu bar. Then, click **Header/Footer**. This selects the Layout Header/Footer command. WordPerfect displays the Headers/Footers dialog box. Header A is selected. Click **Create**.

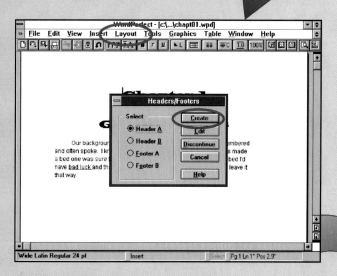

NOTE ▼

You can create a second header or footer by selecting Header B or Footer B in the Headers/Footers dialog box. You might, for example, create one header for odd pages and a second header for even pages.

3 You see the Header window and the Header button bar at the top of the Header window.

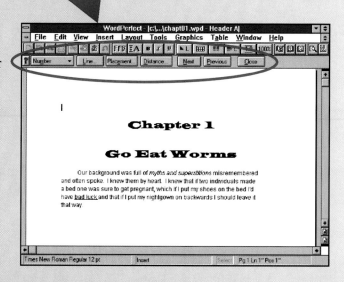

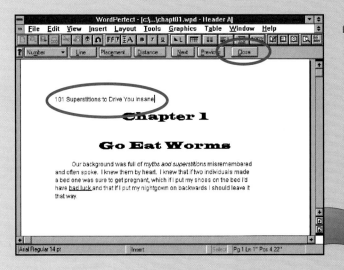

4 Type **101 Superstitions to Drive You Insane** in the Header area. This is the text you want to print at the top of each page. Click **Close** on the Header button bar.

5 This confirms the header and closes the Header window. The header is inserted into your document.

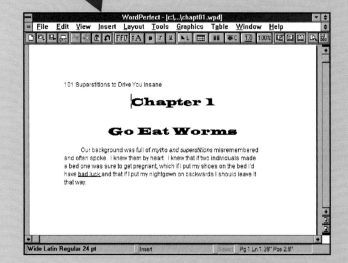

NOTE ▼

The steps for inserting footers are similar to the steps for inserting headers.

WHY WORRY?

If something unexpected prints at the top or bottom of your document, check the Header or Footer window. To delete the header or footer, turn on Reveal Codes (press Alt+F3); then delete the Header or Footer code.

NOTE ▼

To include page numbers in the header or footer, choose Number Page Number.

TASK 49

Editing a Header or Footer

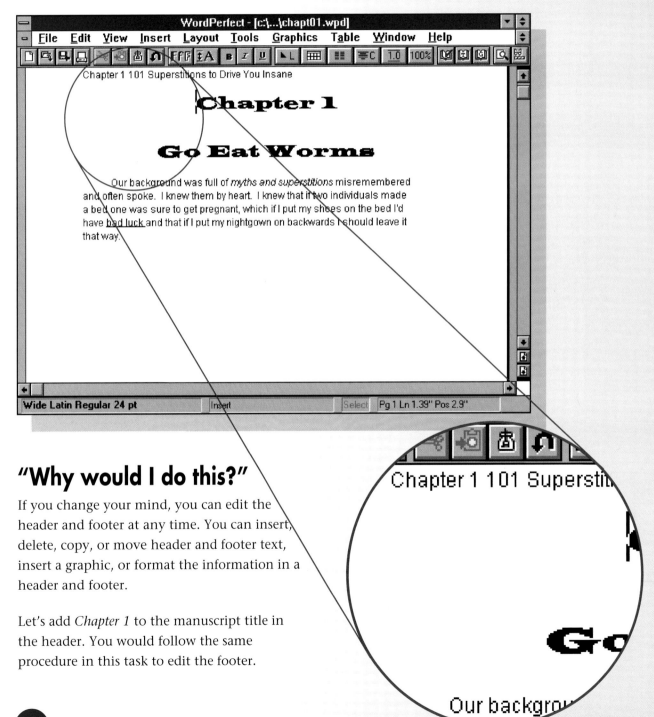

"Why would I do this?"

If you change your mind, you can edit the header and footer at any time. You can insert, delete, copy, or move header and footer text, insert a graphic, or format the information in a header and footer.

Let's add *Chapter 1* to the manuscript title in the header. You would follow the same procedure in this task to edit the footer.

1 Click **Layout** in the menu bar; then click **Header/Footer**. The Headers/Footers dialog box appears. Click Edit to open the Header A window. The Header button bar appears at the top of the Header window.

2 Type **Chapter 1** in the Header window and press the space bar. This is the additional text you want to print at the top of each page. Click **Close** in the Header window. This confirms the header and closes the Header window.

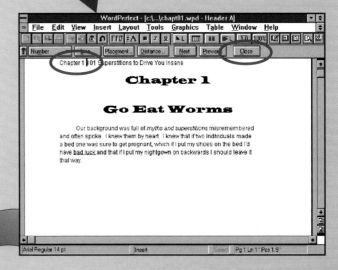

3 On-screen, you cannot see the header change. To do so, you must view the document in Full Page view.

WHY WORRY?

Follow the same procedure to change the header back to its original text. To delete the header, turn on Reveal Codes (press Alt+F3); then delete the Header code.

153

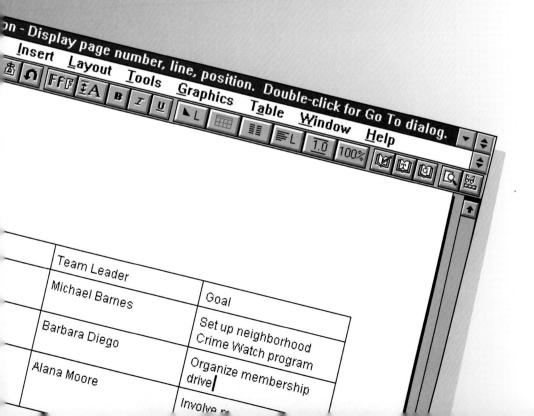

Part VII: Enhancing Your Document

This part shows you how to draw a horizontal line, insert a graphic, move and resize a graphic, and delete a graphic. You also learn how to create a table, enter text in a table, add a row to a table, and delete a row from a table. Finally, you learn how to create a two-column document, and type text into a two-column document.

You can enhance the appearance of a document by drawing emphasis lines anywhere in the document. Once you create the line, you can change the position, thickness, or other aspects of the line. You also can create a custom line.

Adding lines works well on newsletter headings. Horizontal lines also can be used to separate parts of a document, company logos, or invitations. The Sample Documents section at the end of this book contains several documents that have these features.

You can insert graphics to spice up your document. WordPerfect provides clip-art files and supports many import file types and various graphics formats. A WordPerfect graphic image file includes the extension WPG, which stands for WordPerfect graphic. You can insert any graphic image that you created with WordPerfect's drawing feature or a WordPerfect graphic created in another program.

A graphic image must be inserted into a box, which you create before you insert the graphic image.

WordPerfect treats a graphic as an object you can move and resize. You can select the graphic and then move it to a new location in your document, or stretch or shrink the graphics to any shape and size you want. If you no longer want the graphic in your document, you can delete the graphic.

The Tables feature enables you to create a table with columns and rows instantly. Then, you can enter text and numbers (similar to a spreadsheet) in the table without defining tab settings. Once you create the table, you can easily insert and delete rows in the table to suit your needs.

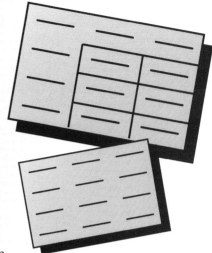

There are several other things you can do to customize a table. You can join cells, split cells, and hide or show the lines in a table. You can even sort text and numbers in a table, create formulas to perform math calculations on numbers in a table, and import a spreadsheet file into a table.

In this part, you learn how to create a two-column document which looks like newspaper-style columns. Newspaper-style columns are sometimes referred to as snaking columns. Snaking columns contain text that wraps from the bottom of one column to the top of the next column. Two-column documents are handy for newspapers, newsletters, bulletins, magazine articles, lists, and indexes.

Once you create the two-column document, you learn how to enter text into the two columns. As you type the text, WordPerfect wraps the text within the column until you reach the bottom of the page and then wraps to the top of the next column.

WordPerfect's Layout Columns Define command enables you to change the column definition of your columns. For example, you can change the number of columns, the type of columns, the space between the columns, the width of the columns, and other options in the Columns dialog box.

You also can move around columns with the cursor movement keys, as well as copy, move, and delete columns.

This part shows you the formatting operations you need for enhancing the appearance and layout of your documents.

TASK 50
Drawing a Horizontal Line

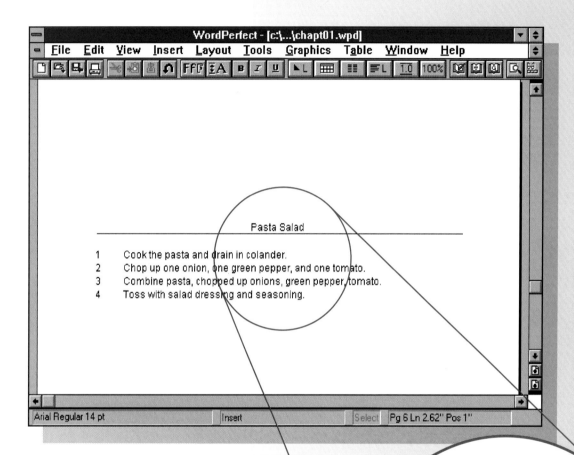

"Why would I do this?"

WordPerfect's Graphics Horizontal Line feature enables you to add a horizontal line at the top or bottom of paragraphs. For example, you can have a single line beneath the title of a newsletter to bring attention to it.

In your manuscript document, add a horizontal line beneath the title at the top of page 6 to draw attention to it.

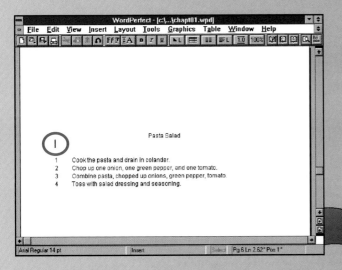

1 Scroll to page 6. Select the title *Pasta Salad*. Click **Justification** in the Power Bar and choose **Center** to center the text. Click at the beginning of the next line (blank line) below the centered text. This blank line is where you want to insert the horizontal line.

2 Click **Graphics** in the menu bar. This opens the Graphics menu. You see a list of Graphics commands. Click **Horizontal Line**. This selects the Horizontal Line command.

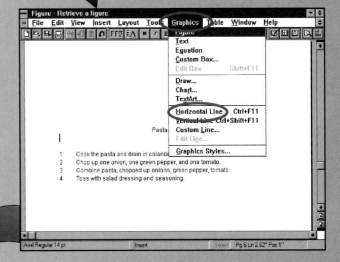

NOTE ▼

You also can press Ctrl+F11 to select the Graphics Horizontal Line command.

3 A default line is created automatically.

WHY WORRY?

To delete the line, immediately click the Undo button on the Power Bar. Or turn on Reveal Codes (press Alt+F3); then delete the Graph Line code.

TASK 51
Inserting a Graphic

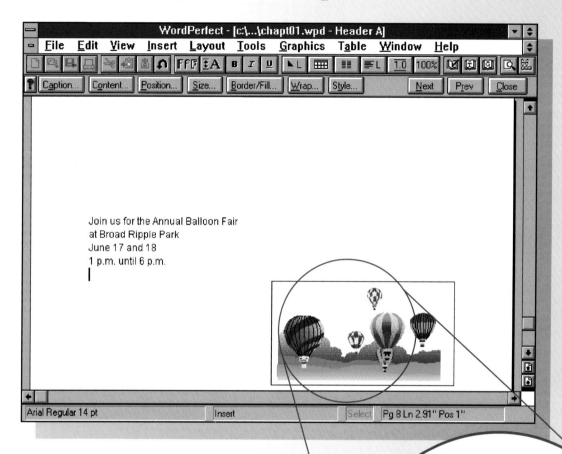

"Why would I do this?"

WordPerfect lets you insert graphics in your document to add emphasis and visual impact. Graphics can liven up any document. ·

Let's type an invitation to a balloon fair. Then, we will insert a graphic of hot air balloons next to the invitation.

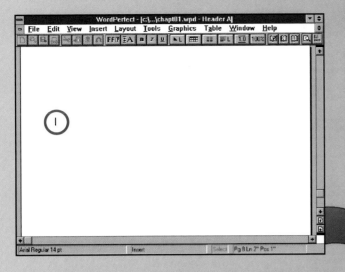

1 Press **Ctrl+End** or scroll to the bottom of the document. Then, press **Ctrl+Enter** to insert a page break.

2 On page 8, type the text that appears in the figure so that your screen matches the screen in the book.

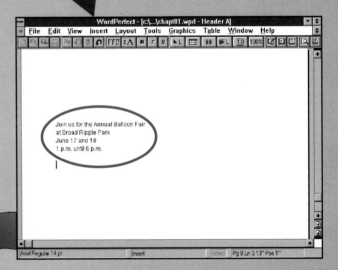

3 Click **Graphics** in the menu bar; then click **Figure**. You see the Insert Image dialog box. The graphics files in the files list appear in the dialog box.

Task 51: Inserting a Graphic

4 In the files list, scroll down until you see **hotair.wpg**. Click it. This selects the graphic that you want to insert. Click **OK**.

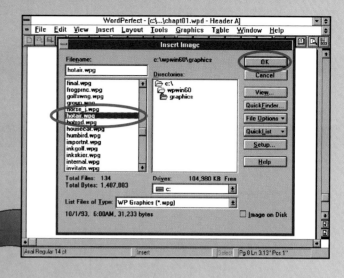

5 The graphic is inserted on-screen in the default position and size. (In the next task, you learn to change the box position and size.)

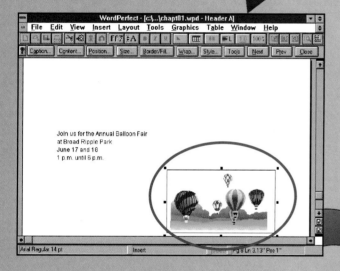

6 Click outside the graphic. This step deselects the graphic.

WHY WORRY?

To undo the graphic insertion, click Undo in the Power Bar immediately. Or turn on Reveal Codes (press Alt+F3); then delete the Box code.

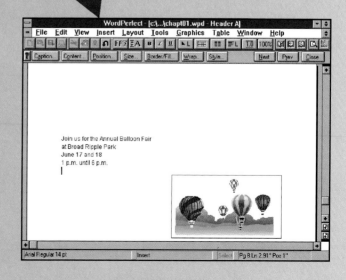

Moving and Resizing a Graphic

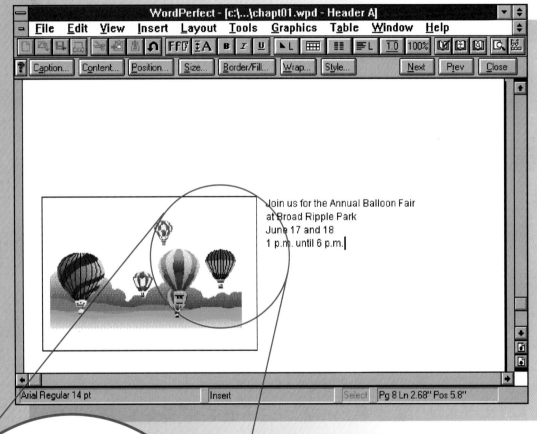

"Why would I do this?"

Once you've inserted a graphic in your document, you may need to move or resize it. If you think that the graphic would look better in a different area, you can move the graphic to the new location. If you want to shrink the graphic or make it taller and wider, you can resize the graphic.

First we move the hot air balloons, and then we resize the butterfly.

Task 52: Moving and Resizing a Graphic

1 Click the graphic. This selects the graphic you want to move. A dotted rectangle surrounds the graphic, and selection handles appear next to the graphic. A four-headed arrow appears when the mouse pointer is positioned on the graphic.

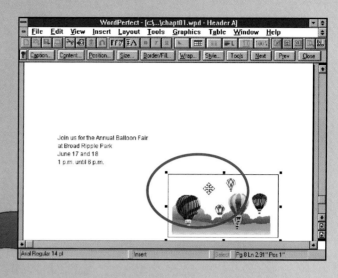

2 Hold down the mouse button and drag the graphic to the left side of the screen. Then release the mouse button. This moves the graphic to the new location.

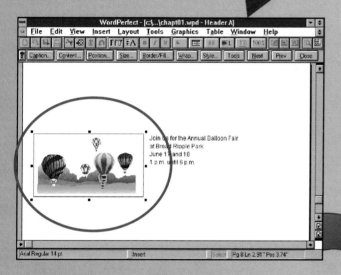

3 To resize the graphic, move the mouse pointer to the bottom middle selection handle, and when the cursor changes to a double-headed arrow, click and hold down the mouse button and drag the graphic down about 1/2 inch. This makes the graphic taller.

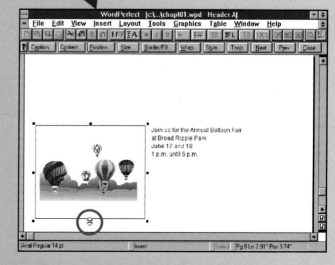

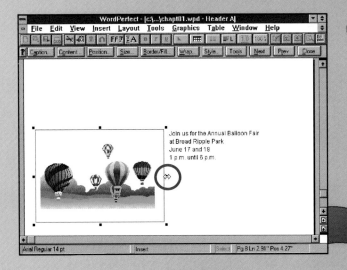

4 Move the mouse pointer to the right middle selection handle and when the cursor changes to a double-headed arrow, drag the graphic to the right about 1/2 inch. This makes the graphic wider.

5 Click outside the graphic. This deselects the graphic.

WHY WORRY?

Follow the same procedures to move the graphic back to its original location, or to change the graphic back to its original size.

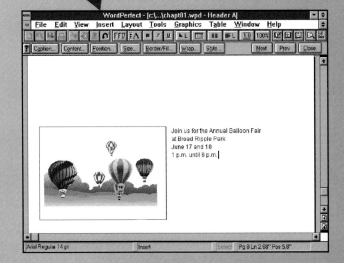

Creating a Table

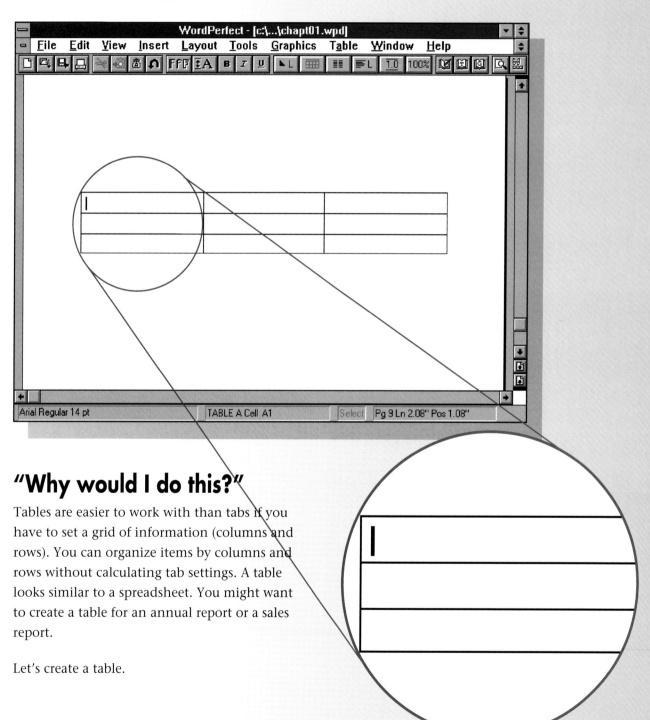

"Why would I do this?"

Tables are easier to work with than tabs if you have to set a grid of information (columns and rows). You can organize items by columns and rows without calculating tab settings. A table looks similar to a spreadsheet. You might want to create a table for an annual report or a sales report.

Let's create a table.

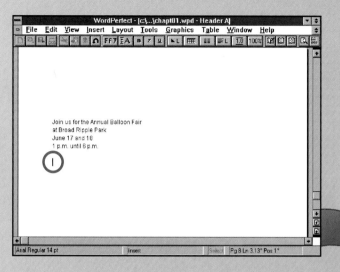

1 Press **Ctrl+End**. This moves the insertion point to the bottom of the document.

2 Press **Ctrl+Enter**. Then scroll down so that only page 9 is on-screen. This inserts a page break and reorients the screen.

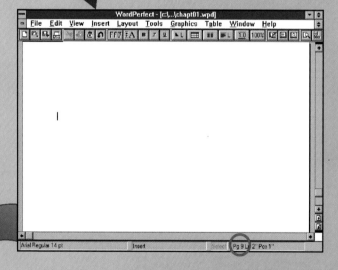

3 Move the mouse pointer to the **Table Quick Create** button (the button that contains a piece of paper with four columns and two rows) on the Power Bar. This moves the mouse pointer to the button you want to select.

4 Click and hold down the mouse button and drag over the grid to highlight three columns and three rows. You see *3 x 3* at the top of the grid. This tells WordPerfect to create a three-column table with three rows.

NOTE ▼

You can always add or delete rows, so don't worry about getting the rows right.

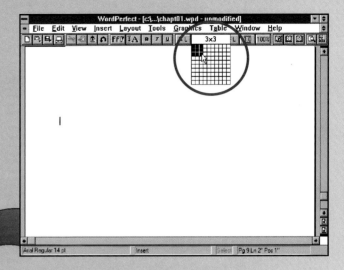

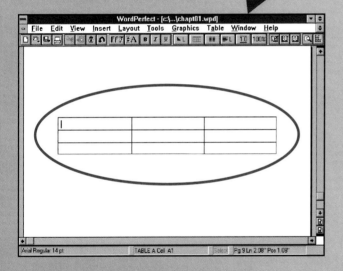

5 Release the mouse button. This confirms the table and inserts a table with three columns and three rows on-screen.

WHY WORRY?

To delete the table, select it and press Delete. Or click the Undo button on the Power Bar immediately.

Entering Text in a Table

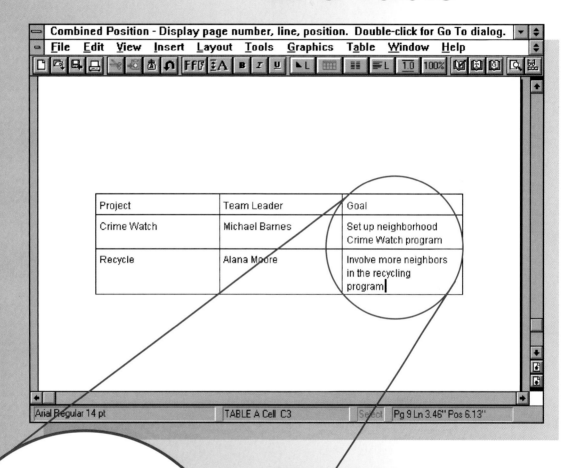

Project	Team Leader	Goal
Crime Watch	Michael Barnes	Set up neighborhood Crime Watch program
Recycle	Alana Moore	Involve more neighbors in the recycling program

Arial Regular 14 pt   TABLE A Cell C3   Select   Pg 9 Ln 3.46" Pos 6.13"

"Why would I do this?"

A WordPerfect table contains columns and rows. The intersection of a row and a column in the table is called a cell. You can enter text in these cells in the table by typing and pressing Tab to move to the next cell.

Let's enter text in your table.

Task 54: Entering Text in a Table

1 Type **Project** and press **Tab**. This enters information into the first cell in the table and moves the insertion point to the next column in that row.

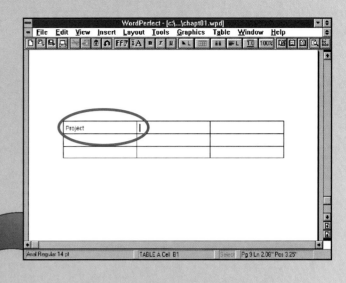

2 Type **Team Leader** and press **Tab**. This enters information in that cell and moves the insertion point to the next column.

3 Type **Goal** and press **Tab**. This completes the headings for the table and moves the insertion point to the first cell in the next row.

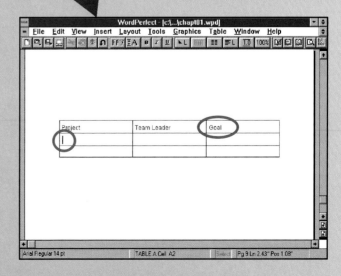

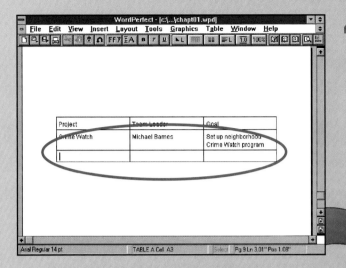

4 Type **Crime Watch** and press **Tab**. Type **Michael Barnes** and press **Tab**. Type **Set up neighborhood Crime Watch program** and press **Tab**. This enters the text for the first row and moves the insertion point to the next row.

5 Type **Recycle** and press **Tab**. Type **Alana Moore** and press **Tab**. Type **Involve more neighbors in the recycling program**. This completes the text for the table.

WHY WORRY?

Make corrections in the table as you would in a normal document. You can press Enter within a table cell to insert a line break.

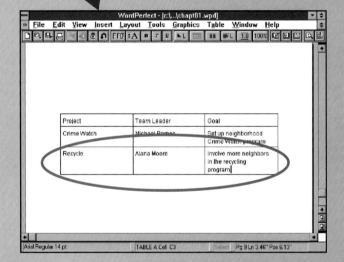

Adding a Row
to a Table

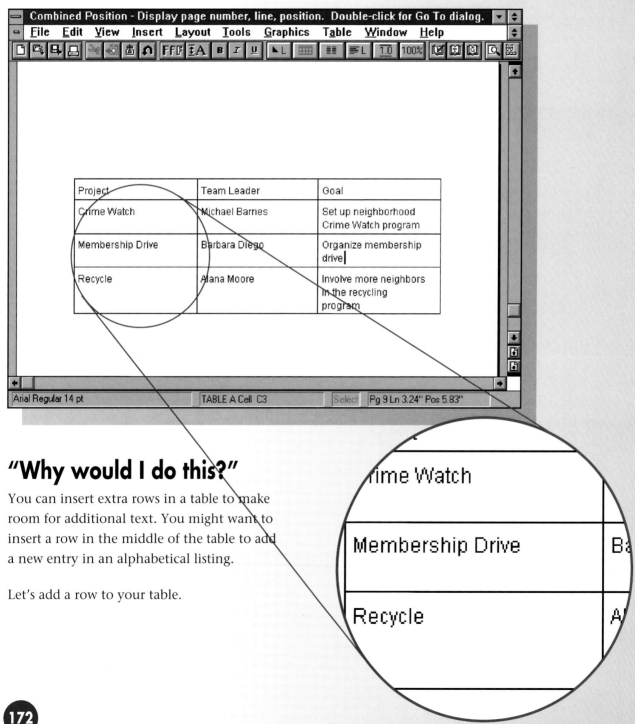

"Why would I do this?"

You can insert extra rows in a table to make room for additional text. You might want to insert a row in the middle of the table to add a new entry in an alphabetical listing.

Let's add a row to your table.

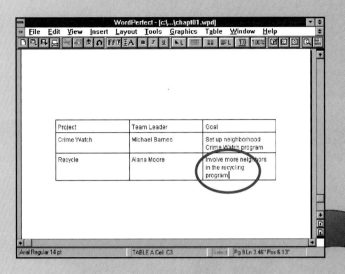

1 Put the insertion point in the last row of the table. (To access the Table commands, you have to put the insertion point within the table.)

2 Click **Table** in the menu bar. Then, click **Insert**. This selects the Table Insert command. You see the Insert Columns/Row dialog box. The Rows options is selected. Click **OK**.

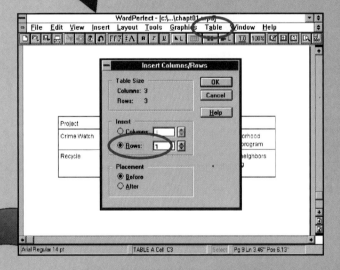

3 A blank row is inserted in the table.

Task 55: Adding a Row to a Table

4 To enter text in the new row, click in the first cell of the new row. Then type **Membership Drive** and press **Tab**.

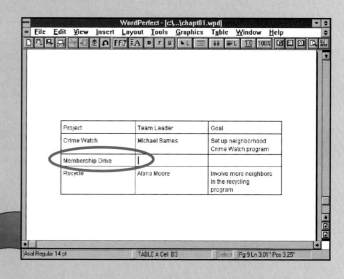

5 Type **Barbara Diego** and press **Tab**. Type **Organize membership drive**. This completes the text for the new row.

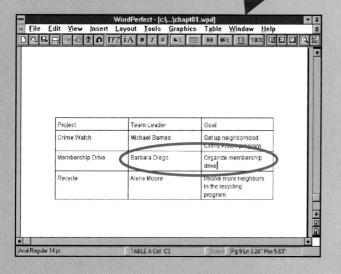

NOTE ▼

As a shortcut, you can put the cursor in the last row and column of the table and press Tab to create a new row at the end of the table.

WHY WORRY?

To undo the change, click the Undo button on the Power Bar. Or delete the row.

Deleting a Row from a Table

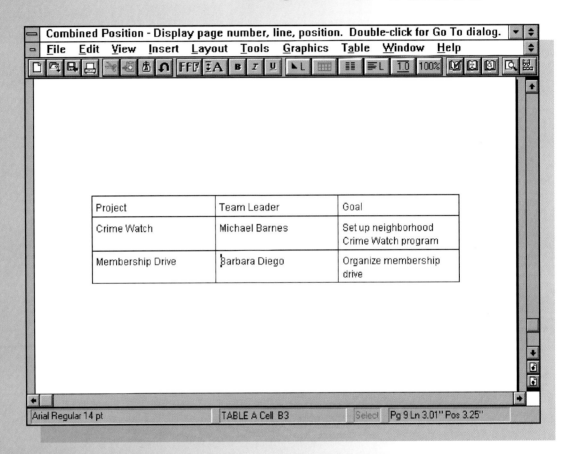

"Why would I do this?"

You might want to delete rows that you no longer want from a table, or you may want to close up some empty space.

Let's delete a row from your table.

Task 56: Deleting a Row from a Table

1 Put the insertion point in the last row of the table. This is the row you want to delete.

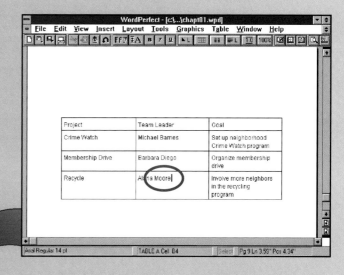

2 Click **Table** in the menu bar. Then, click **Delete**. This step selects the Table Delete command. You see the Delete Columns/Rows dialog box. By default, the Rows option is selected. Click **OK**.

3 This confirms the command. The row is deleted.

WHY WORRY?

To undo the change, click the Undo button on the Power Bar immediately.

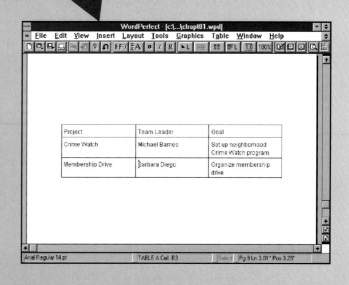

Creating a Two-Column Document

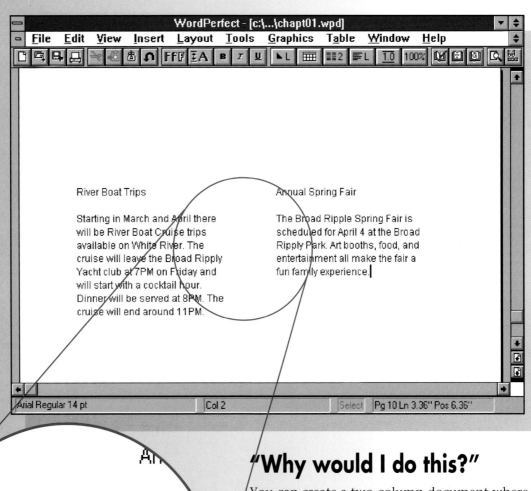

"Why would I do this?"

You can create a two-column document where text flows from one column to the next until all the text is used. Two-column documents work well for newsletters. You also can use columns to create parallel columns for newspapers and magazines, or uneven columns for desktop publishing effects.

Create two columns in your manuscript document. Then type the text into the two columns.

Task 57: Creating a Two-Column Document

1 Press **Ctrl+End**. This step moves the insertion point to the end of the document, where you will insert a page break.

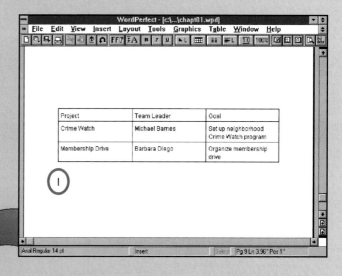

2 Press **Ctrl+Enter**. This inserts a page break. The insertion point is at the top of the new page, where you want to create the columns.

3 Move the mouse pointer to the **Column Define** button (the button with two columns) on the Power Bar.

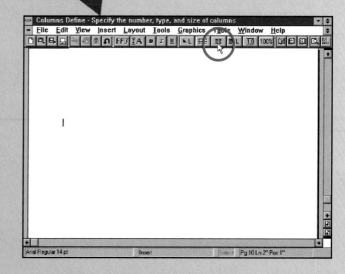

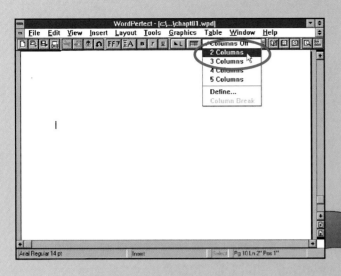

4 Click and hold down the mouse button and drag down to *2 Columns*. This tells WordPerfect to create two columns.

5 Release the mouse button. This accepts the defaults for the other column settings and returns you to the document. There are two changes on-screen: a number 2 is next to the columns on the Columns button and the Col indicator is in the status bar.

WHY WORRY?

To undo the columns, click the Undo button on the Power Bar immediately. Or turn on Reveal Codes (press Alt+F3); then delete the Col Def code.

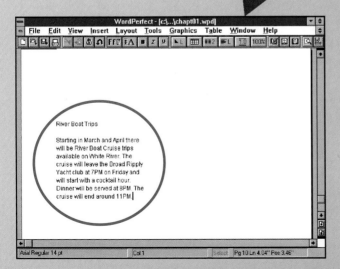

6 Type the text that appears in the figure so that your screen matches the screen in this book. As you type, the text wraps within the column. When the column fills up, the text flows to the next column. This step enters text for the first column.

Task 57: Creating a Two-Column Document

7 Press **Ctrl+Enter**. This inserts a column break and moves the insertion point to the next column. You see the Col 2 indicator in the status bar.

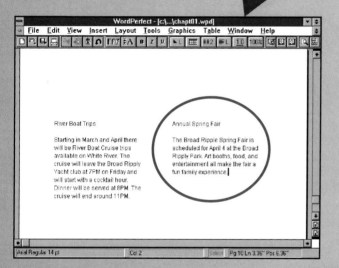

8 Type the text that appears in the figure so that your screen matches the screen in the book. As you type, the text wraps within the column. This step enters text for the second column.

> **NOTE** ▼
>
> Make any editing changes the same way you would in a one-column document. All editing and formatting features work the same in a two-column format as they do in a one-column format.

PART VIII

Viewing and Printing the Document

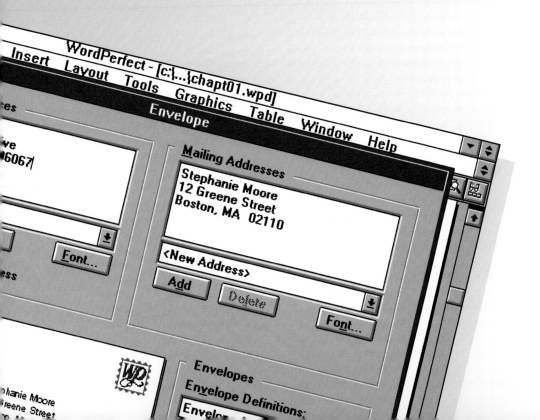

Part VIII: Viewing and Printing the Document

In this part, you learn how to change the view of your document, select a printer, print the document, print selected text, and address an envelope.

The View commands let you see document pages on-screen as they will appear printed on paper, including page numbers, headers, footers, fonts, font sizes and styles, orientation, and margins. Previewing your document is a great way to catch formatting errors, such as incorrect margins, overlapped text, boldfaced text, and other text enhancements. You will save costly printer paper and time by first previewing your document.

You can select different views (100%, 200%), and you can zoom in and out. You also can display full pages and facing pages. Full-Page view enables you to display multiple columns, margin changes, headers and footers, and footnotes in the document.

WordPerfect's Zoom feature lets you enlarge or reduce the view of a page on-screen. Text on-screen can be smaller or larger, and may show the whole page or a smaller section of it at higher magnification. If you want to zoom in for a closer look at your document, select a higher percentage of magnification. If you work with small font sizes, you can inspect the text closely without having to preview or print the worksheet. If you want to zoom out so the whole page shows on-screen at one glance, select a lower percentage of magnification.

WordPerfect's Select Printer feature lets you see the current hardware settings for the printer or printers connected to your computer. These hardware settings are stored in a printer definition. A printer definition tells WordPerfect how to control a certain make and model of printer. You may install and have available for selection an unlimited number of printer definitions.

The first time you use your printer with WordPerfect, it is a good idea to check the Setup options. WordPerfect can use the options and capabilities that are available with each printer. Often, you need to provide more details about your printer so that WordPerfect knows the capabilities available. If you want to specify details about your printer, choose the File Select Printer command and click the Setup button. You then confirm that you installed the right printer and connected it correctly, or you can switch to a different printer.

In WordPerfect, you can print your documents using a basic printing procedure or you can enhance the printout using several page setup options as explained in Part VI, "More Formatting."

It is a good idea to save your documents before printing—just in case a printer error or other problem occurs. You won't lose any work since the last time you saved the document. You learn how to print your document from the Print dialog box. But if you already set up your print options and you're back to the document, you can just click the Print button on the Power Bar to print your document.

In WordPerfect, the Print dialog box lets you print some or all the pages within a document, the current page, multiple pages, selected text, and multiple copies of the printout. The Document settings control options such as text and graphics quality.

WordPerfect gives you two ways to print addresses on envelopes. If you want to print addresses on envelopes individually, use the Envelope command. WordPerfect will print the return address and the mailing address on the envelope. If you want to print many envelopes at one time, you can use the Merge feature to do a mass mailing.

This part introduces you to the basics of printing the document. With some experimentation and practice, you will be able to create some very interesting print results.

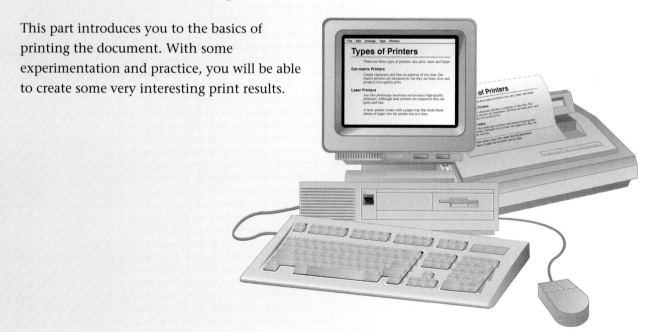

TASK 58

Displaying a Document in Page Layout View

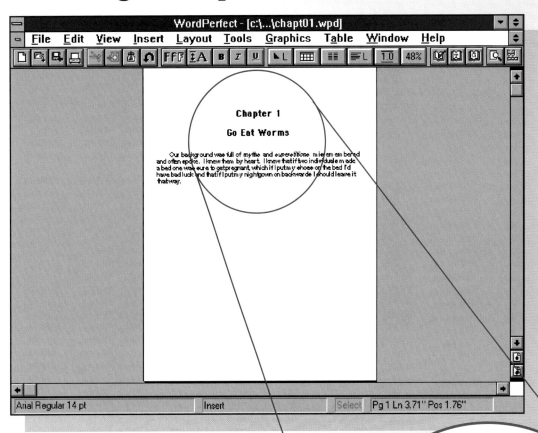

"Why would I do this?"

Full Page view lets you view your document as it will be printed, while retaining all editing features and capabilities (unlike Print Preview). This feature is useful when you are making many formatting changes and need to see the results.

Let's display our CHAPT01.WPD document in Full Page view.

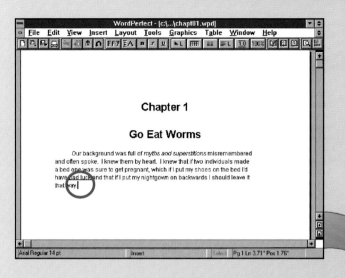

1 Press **Ctrl+Home** to go to page 1. This places the insertion point on the page you want to preview.

2 Click **View** in the menu bar. This opens the View menu, where you see a list of View commands. Click **Zoom**.

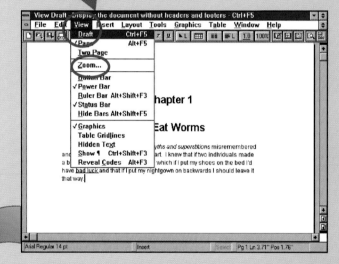

3 This selects the Zoom command. You see the Zoom dialog box that contains a list of Zoom options.

4 Click the **Full-Page** option button. This selects the Full-Page option. Click **OK**.

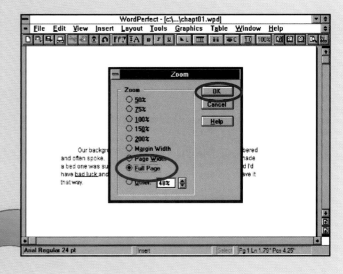

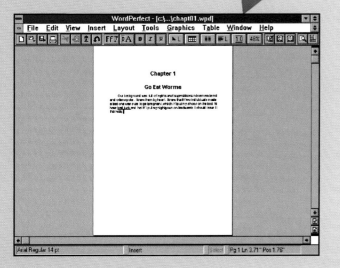

5 You see the document in Full-Page view. As you can see, the effect of margin changes appear in this view.

WHY WORRY?

To turn off Full-Page view, you must select another view. To return to 100% view, follow the same procedure, but select 100% instead of Full-Page.

TASK 59

Viewing Two Pages On-Screen

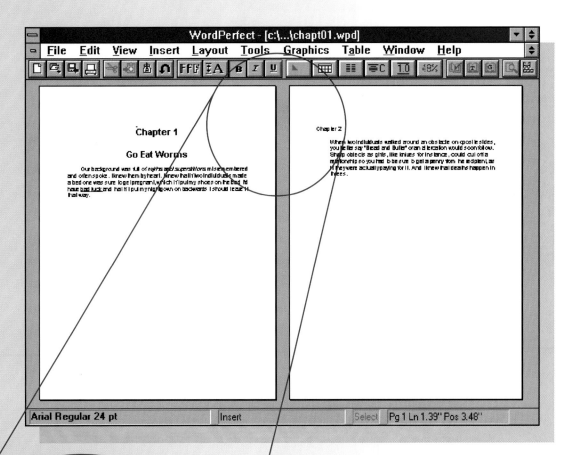

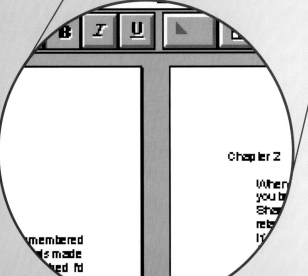

"Why would I do this?"

WordPerfect's Two Page feature enables you to view facing pages. That way, you can see a thumbnail sketch of the two pages. This view is useful if you are creating a manuscript. You can get a feel for the layout of both pages together.

Let's examine how to view page 1 and page 2 as two facing pages.

Task 59: Viewing Two Pages On-Screen

1 Press **Ctrl+Home**. This step reorients the screen.

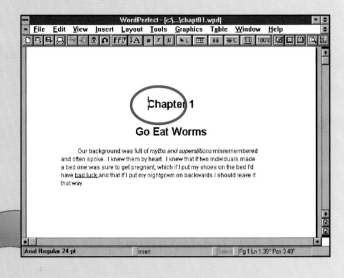

2 Click **View** in the menu bar; then click **Two Page**. This selects the View Two Page command where you see two pages on-screen.

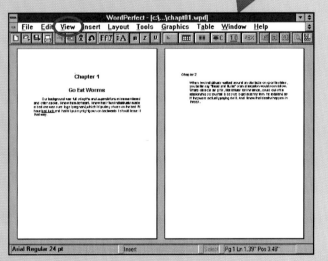

WHY WORRY?

Choose View Page to return to the normal view.

Selecting a Printer

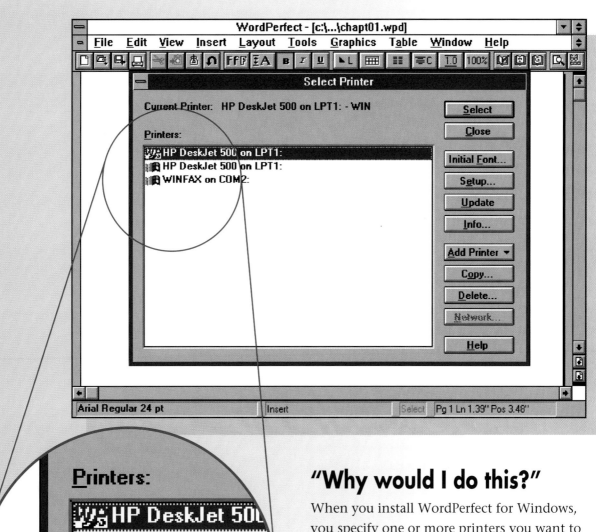

"Why would I do this?"

When you install WordPerfect for Windows, you specify one or more printers you want to use with the program. You can easily change the printer setup when you want to specify a different printer or to take advantage of all your printer's capabilities. The printer uses any special formatting you specify in addition to any printer options you specify.

Let's select a printer.

Task 60: Selecting a Printer

1 Click **File** in the menu bar; then click **Select Printer**. This selects the File Select Printer command. You see the Select Printer dialog box that displays the current printer and lists available printers. The currently selected printer is highlighted.

NOTE ▼

For information on all dialog box options, see your WordPerfect for Windows documentation.

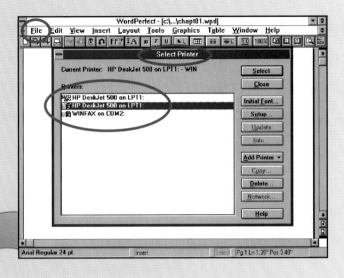

2 Click the printer you want to use. We chose HP DeskJet 500 on LPT1. This selects the printer you are using. Click **Select**. This chooses the Select button and tells WordPerfect to use the selected printer to print documents.

WHY WORRY?

To close the dialog box without making a change, click the Close button or press Esc.

3 The dialog box closes, and you return to your document.

NOTE ▼

Your printer selection also affects what fonts are available.

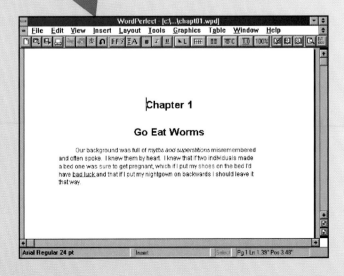

Printing Your Document

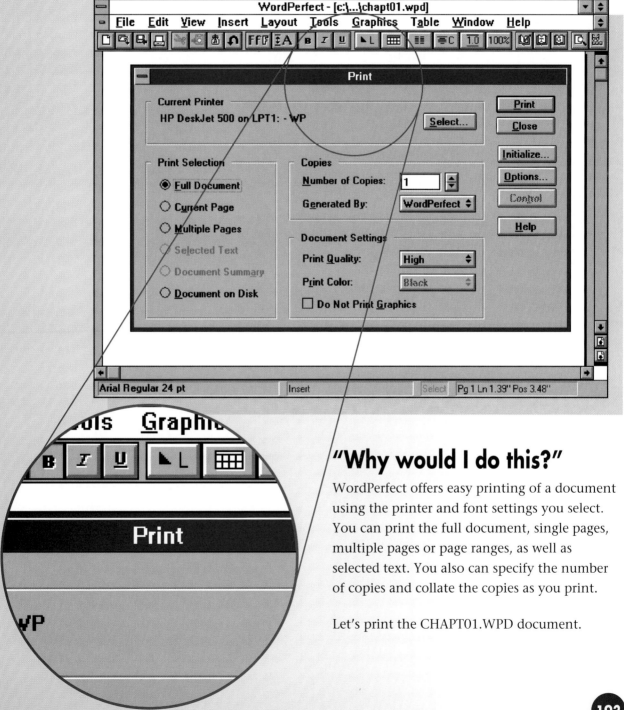

"Why would I do this?"

WordPerfect offers easy printing of a document using the printer and font settings you select. You can print the full document, single pages, multiple pages or page ranges, as well as selected text. You also can specify the number of copies and collate the copies as you print.

Let's print the CHAPT01.WPD document.

193

Task 61: Printing Your Document

1 Click **File** in the menu bar. Then, click **Print**. This selects the File Print command. WordPerfect opens the Print dialog box. You see the name of your printer at the top of the dialog box. This dialog box enables you to control what you print, how many copies you print, and other options.

NOTE ▼

You also can press F5 to select the Print command or click the Print button on the Power Bar.

2 Click **Print** to start printing the document.

NOTE ▼

When you installed the WordPerfect program, you also installed the printer. If no printer is installed, refer to the WordPerfect for Windows manual.

WHY WORRY?

While the document is printing, you see a Current Print Job dialog box on-screen that lists the print status. To stop the print job, click Cancel Print Job or press Esc.

Printing
Selected Text

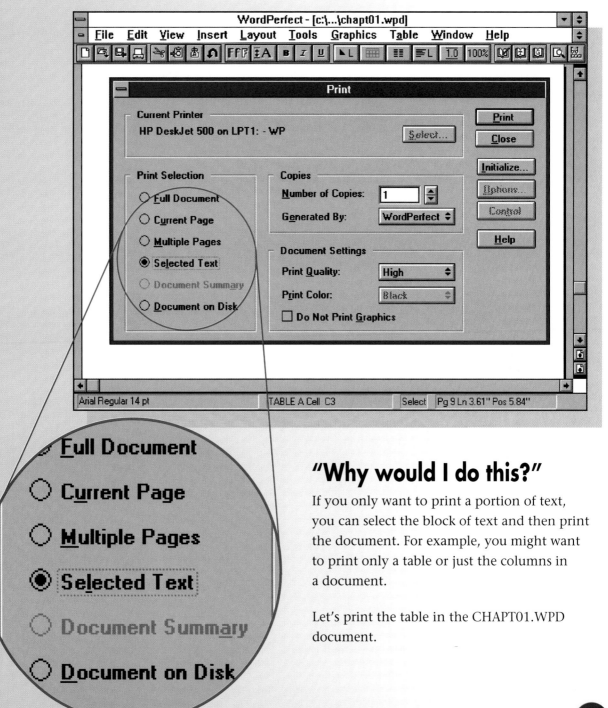

"Why would I do this?"

If you only want to print a portion of text, you can select the block of text and then print the document. For example, you might want to print only a table or just the columns in a document.

Let's print the table in the CHAPT01.WPD document.

Task 62: Printing Selected Text

1 Scroll to page 9. Select the entire table. This selects the text you want to print.

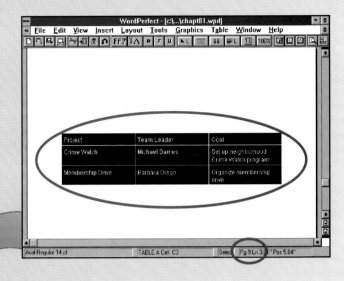

2 Click **File** in the menu bar; then click **Print**. This selects the File Print command. WordPerfect opens the Print dialog box. The Selected Text option button is selected in the Print Selection area of the dialog box.

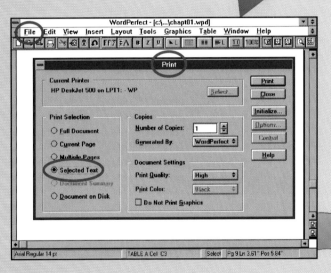

NOTE ▼

You also can press F5 to select the Print command or click the Print button on the Power Bar.

3 Click **Print** to start printing the document.

WHY WORRY?

While the document is printing, you see a Current Print Job dialog box on-screen that lists the print status. To stop the print job, click Cancel Print Job.

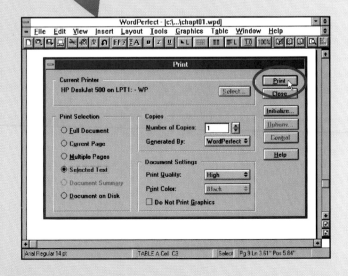

Addressing an Envelope

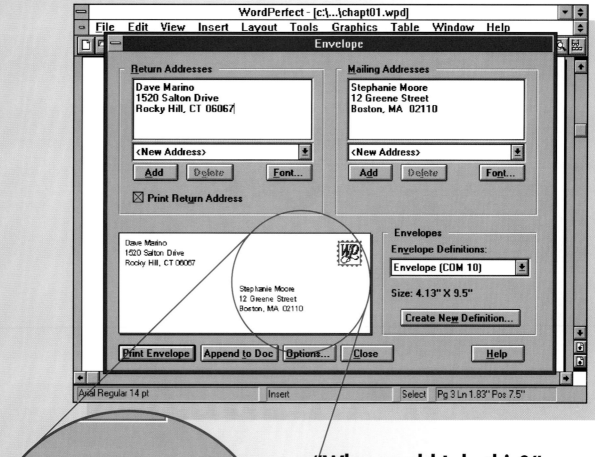

"Why would I do this?"

WordPerfect's Envelope feature lets you print addresses on envelopes individually. You can print the return address and the mailing address on the envelope. In order to use this feature, you must have a printer that can print on envelopes.

Let's print the mailing address on an envelope in the CHAPT01.WPD document.

Task 63: Addressing an Envelope

1 Scroll to page 3. Select the mailing address. This selects the address you want to print on an envelope.

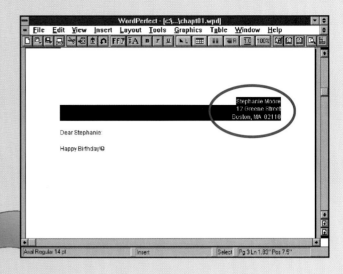

2 Click **Layout** in the menu bar; then click **Envelope**. This selects the Layout Envelope command. WordPerfect opens the Envelope dialog box. This dialog box enables you to select an envelope size, specify a return address, a mailing address, and other options. Notice the address you selected in the document appears in the Mailing Addresses text box. The insertion point is in the Return Addresses text box.

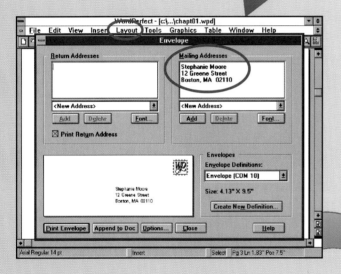

3 Type the return address that appears in the figure so that your screen matches the computer screen in the book. Next, insert your envelope into the printer. Then, click the **Print Envelope** button to start printing the address on an envelope.

WHY WORRY?

If you change your mind, click Close to close the dialog box without printing an address on the envelope.

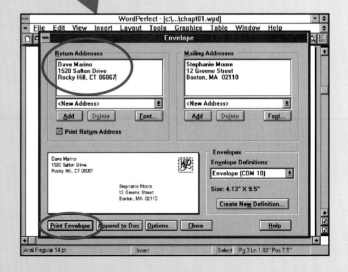

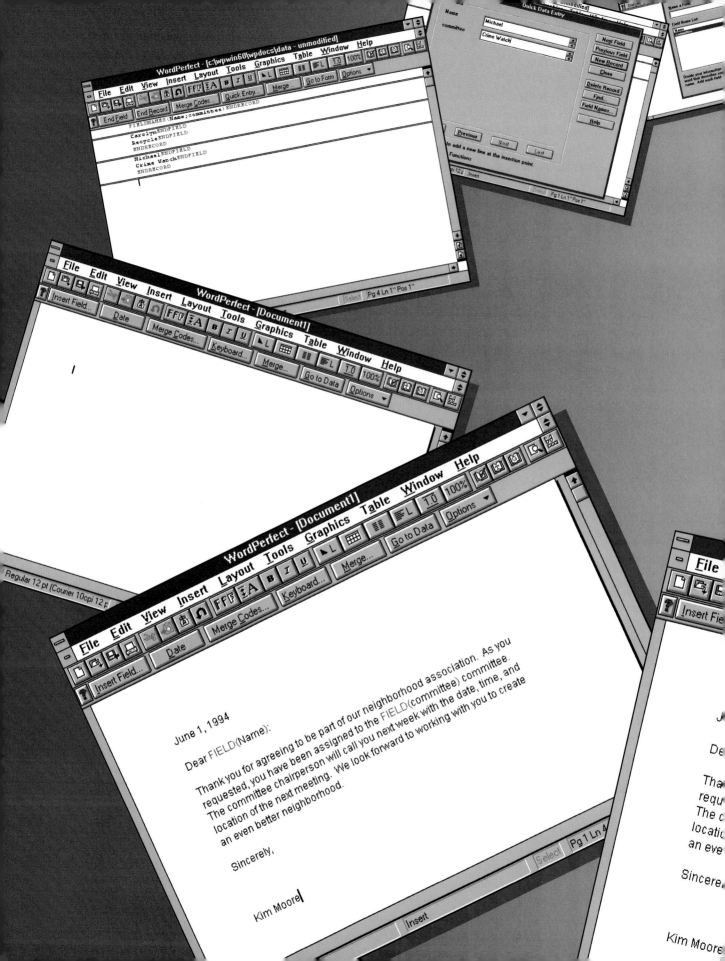

PART IX
Merging

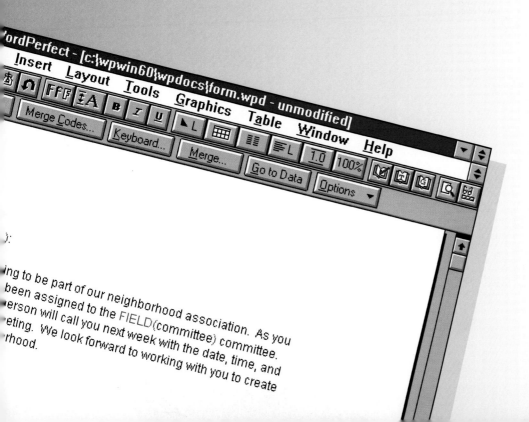

Part IX: Merging

In this part, you learn how to create a merge letter, which is an involved process. The tasks in this part all build on each other and follow one right after the other. You should follow all the tasks in the section to complete the merge process.

Two files make up a basic merge procedure: the data file and the form file. The *data file* contains the field definition and the variable information you want inserted into the form file. The *form file* contains the unchanging text and the codes that control the merge.

There are several tasks you must follow to create a merge letter. First you create the data file. Next you create the form file. You create your own fields that you can use in the data file.

You then save the data file. After you save the data file, you enter records. A *record* is one set of information. Each individual element in the record is stored in a field. You will create a document—with the specific information in that record—for each record you enter.

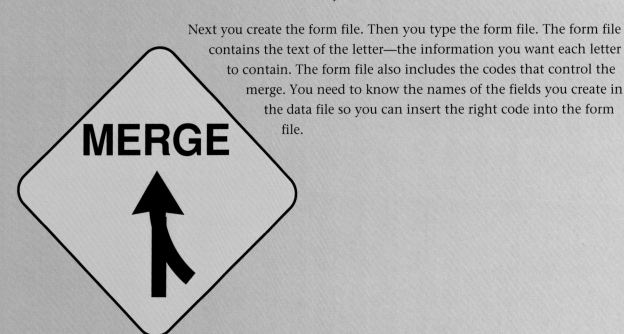

Next you create the form file. Then you type the form file. The form file contains the text of the letter—the information you want each letter to contain. The form file also includes the codes that control the merge. You need to know the names of the fields you create in the data file so you can insert the right code into the form file.

After you create the form file, you save the file. The final step is to merge the two files. A new file will be created that contains a letter for each record in the data source. You can save the new file or print it.

With Merge, you can create form letters for mass mailings, product announcements, customer letters, reports, invitations, and contribution solicitations. You also can merge a list of names and addresses to create invoices and mailing labels, envelopes, and to fill in standard forms. You can, for example, print a phone list, customer list, and even print addresses on envelopes.

WordPerfect's Merge feature offers many options; it can be a pretty complex feature. This book covers the simplest example. If you want more information, see your WordPerfect for Windows documentation.

Creating a Data File

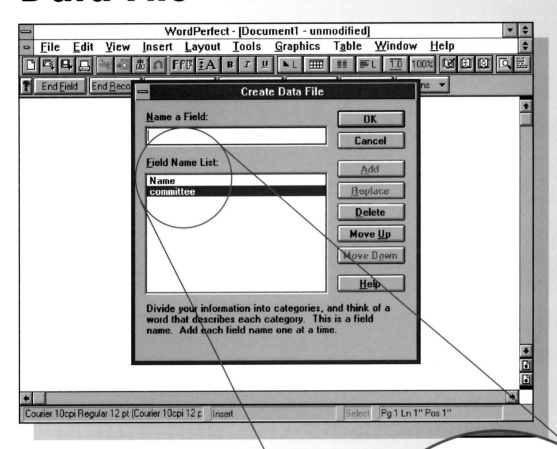

"Why would I do this?"

The data file stores the variable information that you want to insert into the form file. Each piece of information is stored in a field; a set of information is called a record. Perhaps you want to create a data file of addresses for batch mailing.

Let's create a data file. Then, you save the data file. After you save the file, you enter the records in the next task.

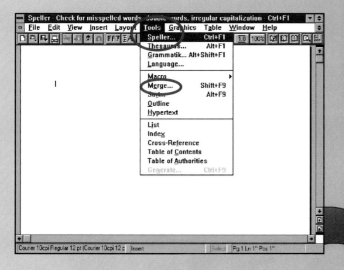

1 From a blank screen, click **Tools** in the menu bar. This opens the Tools menu. You see a list of Tools commands. Click **Merge**.

2 This selects the Merge command and displays the Merge dialog box. Click **Data**. This selects the Data file option.

> **NOTE** ▼
>
> You also can press Shift+F9 to select the Tools Merge command.

3 You see the Create Data File dialog box. The insertion point is in the Name a Field text box.

4 Type **Name**. This enters the name for the first field in the Name a Field text box. Next, click **Add**. This selects the Add button. The field name is added to the Field Name List.

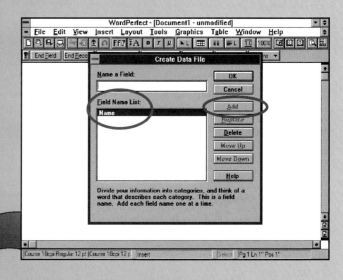

5 Type **committee**. This enters the next field name in the Name a Field text box. Click **Add**. This adds the second field. You can add as many fields as you need. This example only uses two fields. Click **OK**. This completes the Field Name List.

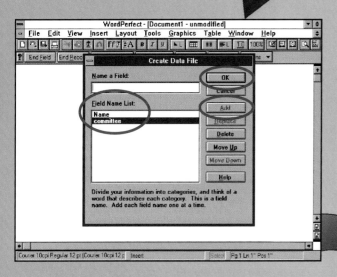

6 You see the Quick Data Entry dialog box. The next task covers entering records using this dialog box.

WHY WORRY?

If you don't want to create the data file, click Cancel or press Esc.

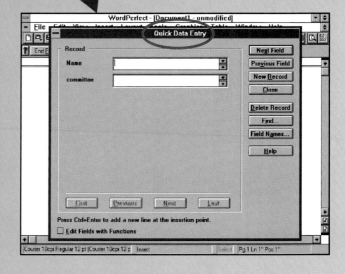

Entering a Record into the Data File

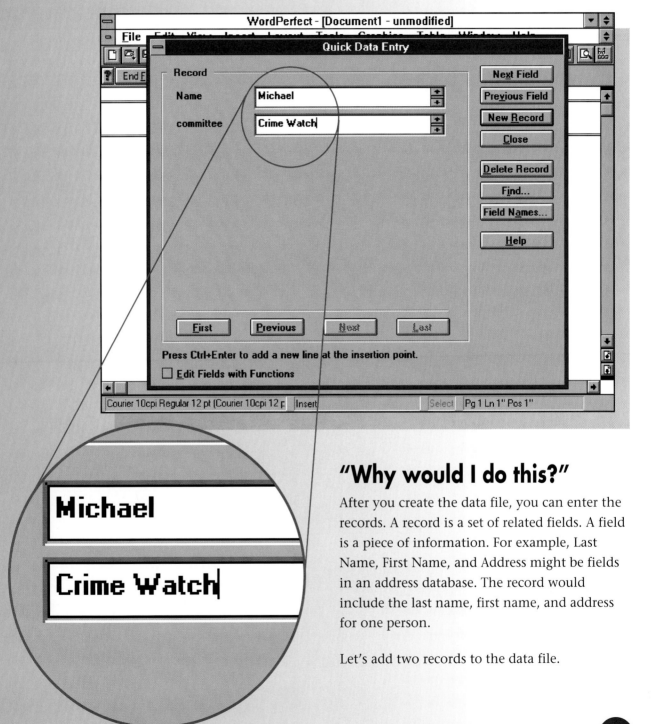

"Why would I do this?"

After you create the data file, you can enter the records. A record is a set of related fields. A field is a piece of information. For example, Last Name, First Name, and Address might be fields in an address database. The record would include the last name, first name, and address for one person.

Let's add two records to the data file.

Task 65: Entering a Record into the Data File

1 Type **Carolyn**. This enters the information for the first field—in this case, the Name field. When you merge the documents, this specific text will be inserted into the document.

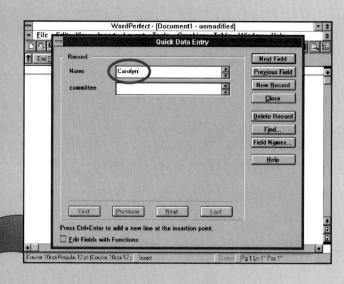

2 Press **Tab**. This moves the insertion point to the committee text box. Type **Recycle**. This enters the specific committee for this person. This information (the name and committee) is stored in a record.

WHY WORRY?

If you make a mistake while typing, correct it as you would in any other document.

3 Click **New Record**. This selects the New Record button. The current record is added to the document; you may be able to see the information behind the dialog box. The text boxes are empty so that you can enter the next record.

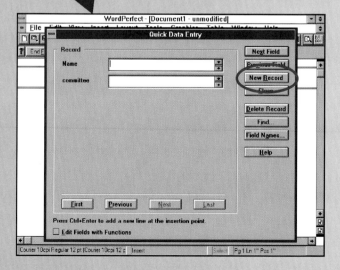

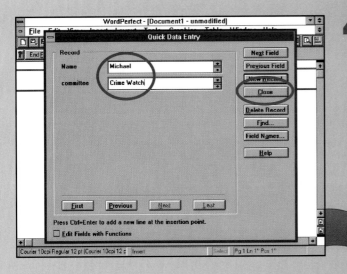

4 Type **Michael**. This enters the information in the first field of the second record. Next, press **Tab**. This moves the insertion point to the next field. Now, type **Crime Watch**. This enters the information for the next field. Click **Close**. This selects the Close button and adds the record to the data document.

5 WordPerfect asks you, Save changes to disk? Click **Yes**. You see the Save Data File As dialog box. This box is similar to the Save As dialog box. The insertion point is in the Filename text box.

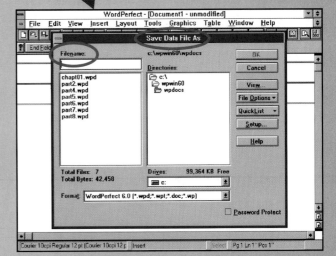

> **NOTE** ▼
>
> To delete a record, use the First, Previous, Next, and Last buttons at the bottom of the Quick Data Entry dialog box to display the record you want. Then click the Delete Record button.

Saving the Data File

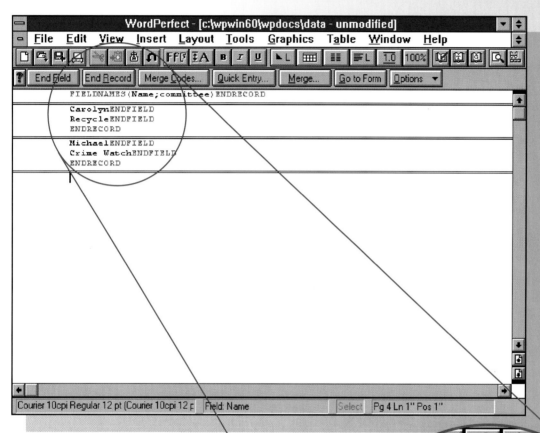

"Why would I do this?"

After you create the data file, you must save the file. As you add records, you should periodically save the file. Select File Save or press Ctrl+S to save the file.

Let's save the data file.

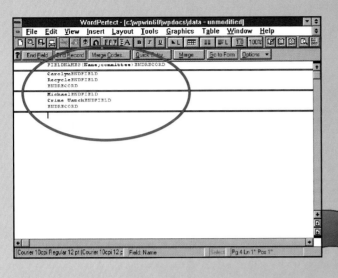

1 Type **DATA**. This enters the name for the data file. The current directory is C:\WPWIN60\WPDOCS. That is where the file will be saved. Next, click **OK**. This saves the document. The document remains open on-screen and the file name—along with the path—appears in the title bar.

WHY WORRY?

If you don't want to save the file, click Cancel.

2 Click **File** in the menu bar. This opens the File menu. You see a list of File commands. Click **Close**.

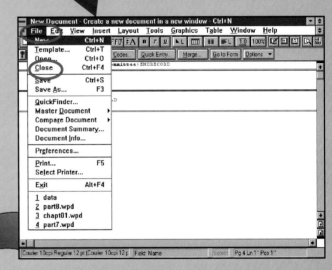

3 This closes the data file so that you can create the next file—the form file.

Creating a Form File

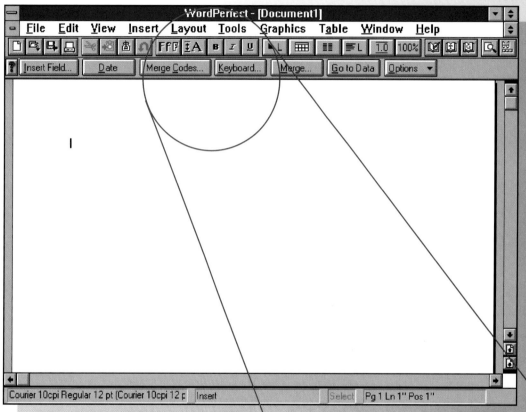

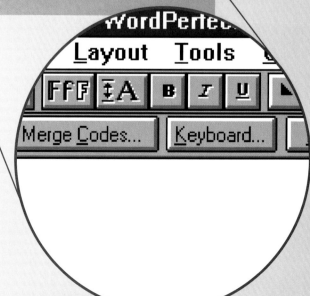

"Why would I do this?"

Before you can merge files, you must create a form file. The form file contains field names and the information that remains constant. Each field name corresponds to a field name in the data file. You might want to create a form file that contains an invitation, a product announcement, or a price list.

Let's create a form file now. Later you will type the text in the form file.

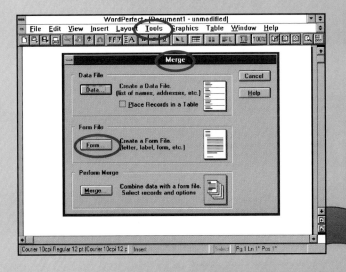

1 Click **Tools** in the menu bar. This opens the Tools menu and displays a list of Tools commands. Next, click **Merge**. This selects the Merge command and displays the Merge dialog box. Click **Form**. This selects the Form file.

NOTE ▼

You also can press Shift+F9 to select the Tools Merge command.

2 You see the Create Form File dialog box. The Associated Data File option button is selected; the insertion point is in the text box. Type **DATA.WPD**. This enters the name of the data file. Next, click **OK**.

3 This creates the file. You see a blank document on-screen. The Merge tools appear along the top of the window. Next, you will type the letter and insert the fields you want; see the next task.

WHY WORRY?

If you don't want to create the form file, click Cancel.

213

Typing a Form File

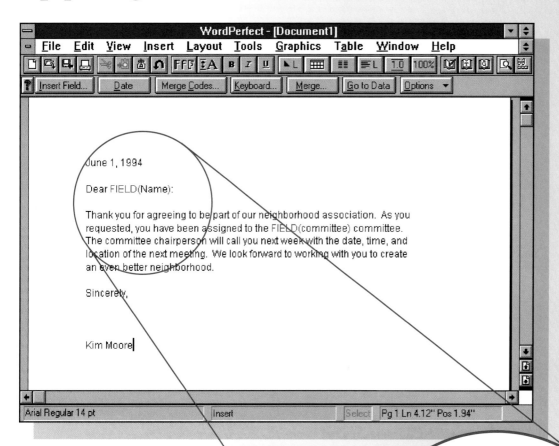

"Why would I do this?"

After you enter the records in the data file and create the form file, you can type the form file. The form file contains the unchanging text and the merge codes that tell WordPerfect where to insert the changing—or variable—information.

Let's type a letter into the form file now.

1 Type **June 1, 1994** and press **Enter** twice. Type **Dear** and press the **space bar**. This enters the beginning text for the form file.

WHY WORRY?

If you make a mistake while typing, correct it as you would in any regular document.

2 Click **Insert Field**. This selects the Insert Field button and displays the Insert Field Name or Number dialog box. You see a list of field names.

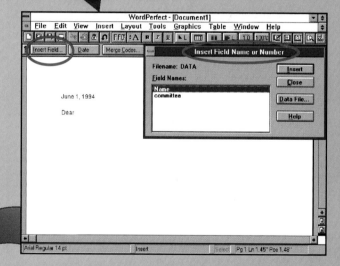

3 Click **Name**, and then click the **Insert** button. This inserts the field name *Name*. On-screen you see the field code. This code tells WordPerfect to insert the information into the first field of each record. You are returned to the document; the dialog box remains open, but not active.

Task 68: Typing a Form File

4 Type : and press **Enter** twice. This finishes the greeting for the letter.

> **NOTE** ▼
>
> If the dialog box covers up the area where you are typing, you can move the dialog box by dragging the box by its title bar.

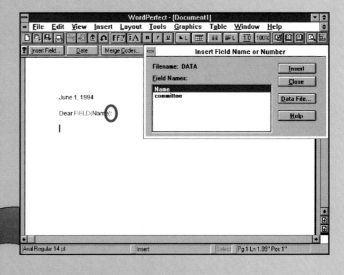

5 Type the middle of the letter: **Thank you for agreeing to be part of our neighborhood association. As you requested, you have been assigned to the**. This enters more of the unchanging text. Be sure to press the **space bar** after *the*.

6 Double-click on **committee** in the Insert Field Name or Number dialog box. This inserts the field name *committee*. On-screen you see the field code. This code tells WordPerfect to insert the information into the second field of each record.

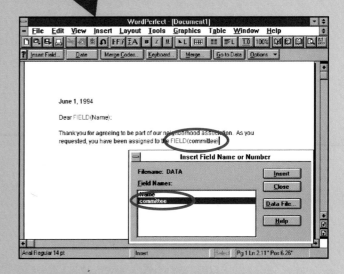

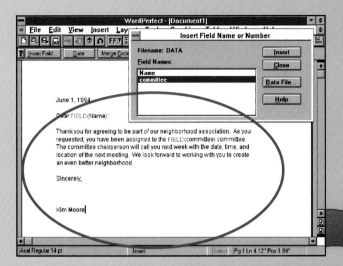

7 Type the rest of the letter: **committee. The committee chairperson will call you next week with the date, time, and location of the next meeting. We look forward to working with you to create an even better neighborhood**. **Sincerely, Kim Moore**

This completes the letter.

8 Click **Close** in the dialog box. This closes the dialog box. Next, save the file, as described in the next task.

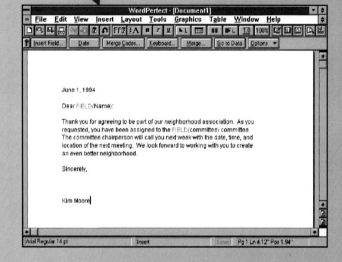

Saving the Form File

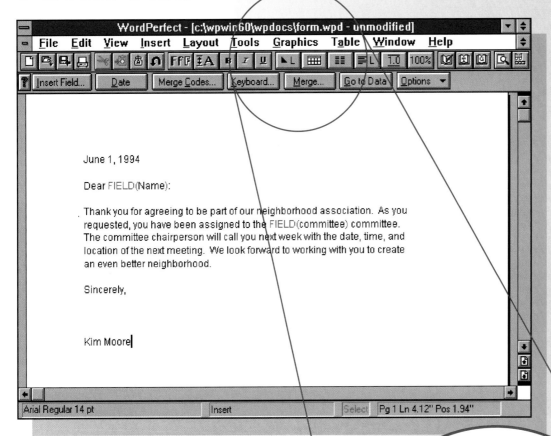

"Why would I do this?"

After you type the form file, you must save the file. Then you can merge the form file and data file. When you work on the form file, you should save often.

Let's save the form file.

1 Click **File** in the menu bar. Then, click **Save**. This selects the File Save command. You see the Save As dialog box. Type **FORM** in the Filename box. This enters the name for the form file. The current directory is C:\WPWIN60\WPDOCS. That is where the file will be saved.

2 Click **OK**. This saves the document. The document remains open on-screen and the file name—along with the path—appears in the title bar.

WHY WORRY?

If you don't want to save the file, click Cancel or press Esc.

3 Click **File** in the menu bar. This opens the File menu. Next, click **Close**. This closes the file. Now you are ready to merge the two files.

Merging the Files

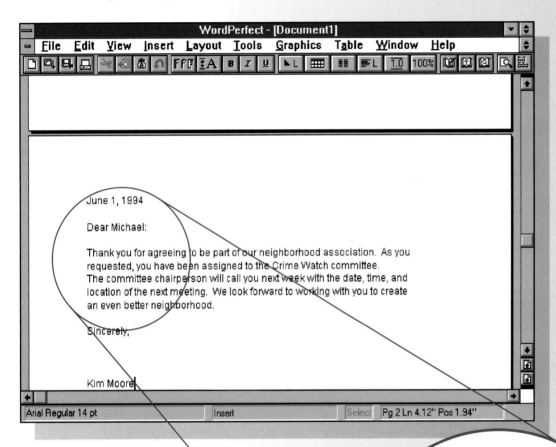

"Why would I do this?"

The last step in the merge process is to merge the main document file and the data source file. WordPerfect creates a new file that contains a letter for each record in the data source. You can save the new file or just print it. The Mail Merge feature offers many options that enable you to control how a merge is performed. If you want more information, see your Microsoft WordPerfect documentation.

Let's merge the two files.

1 Click **Tools** in the menu bar. Then, click **Merge**. This selects the Tools Merge command. You see the Merge dialog box. Click **Merge**. This selects the Merge button.

NOTE ▼

You also can press Shift+F9 to select the Tools Merge command.

2 You see the Perform Merge dialog box. This box contains text boxes in which you type the Form File and Data File names.

3 Type **FORM.WPD** and press **Enter**. This enters the file name for the form document. A unique, specialized letter is created for each record in the data information. You can print or save the letters.

WHY WORRY?

If the merge didn't go as planned, check to be sure that you set up each file correctly.

221

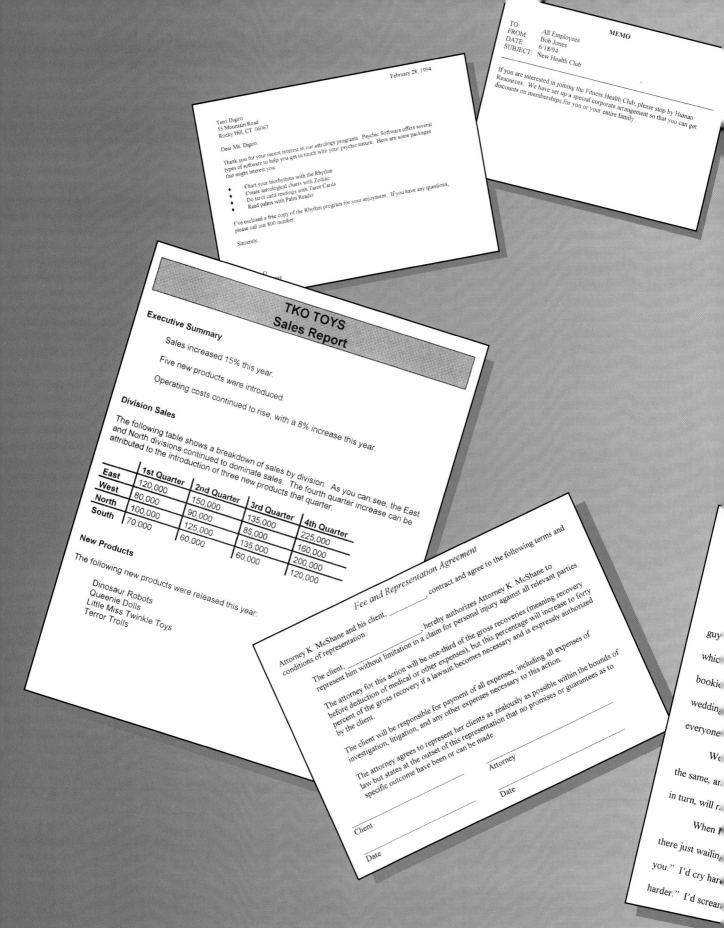

February 28, 1994

Terri Digiro
55 Mountain Road
Rocky Hill, CT 06067

Dear Ms. Digiro:

Thank you for your recent interest in our astrology programs. Psychic Software offers several types of software to help you get in touch with your psychic nature. Here are some packages that might interest you.

- Chart your biorhythms with the Rhythm
- Create astrological charts with Zodiac
- Do tarot card readings with Tarot Cards
- Read palms with Palm Reader

I've enclosed a free copy of the Rhythm program for your enjoyment. If you have any questions, please call our 800 number.

Sincerely,

MEMO

TO: All Employees
FROM: Bob Jones
DATE: 6/18/94
SUBJECT: New Health Club

If you are interested in joining the Fitness Health Club, please stop by Human Resources. We have set up a special corporate arrangement so that you can get discounts on memberships for you or your entire family.

TKO TOYS
Sales Report

Executive Summary

Sales increased 15% this year.

Five new products were introduced.

Operating costs continued to rise, with a 8% increase this year.

Division Sales

The following table shows a breakdown of sales by division. As you can see, the East and North divisions continued to dominate sales. The fourth quarter increase can be attributed to the introduction of three new products that quarter.

	1st Quarter	2nd Quarter	3rd Quarter	4th Quarter
East	120,000	150,000	135,000	225,000
West	80,000	90,000	85,000	160,000
North	100,000	125,000	135,000	200,000
South	70,000	60,000	60,000	120,000

New Products

The following new products were released this year:

Dinosaur Robots
Queenie Dolls
Little Miss Twinkle Toys
Terror Trolls

Fee and Representation Agreement

Attorney K. McShane and his client, _____, contract and agree to the following terms and conditions of representation:

The client, _____, hereby authorizes Attorney K. McShane to represent him without limitation in a claim for personal injury against all relevant parties.

The attorney for this action will be one-third of the gross recoveries (meaning recovery before deduction of medical or other expenses), but this percentage will increase to forty percent of the gross recovery if a lawsuit becomes necessary and is expressly authorized by the client.

The client will be responsible for payment of all expenses, including all expenses of investigation, litigation, and any other expenses necessary to this action.

The attorney agrees to represent her clients as zealously as possible within the bounds of law but states at the outset of this representation that no promises or guarantees as to specific outcome have been or can be made.

_____
Attorney

_____
Date

_____
Client

_____
Date

---

guy

which

bookie

wedding

everyone

We

the same, an

in turn, will r

When

there just wailing

you." I'd cry har

harder." I'd scream

Sample Documents

- ▼ Create a memo
- ▼ Create a business letter
- ▼ Create a report
- ▼ Create a resume
- ▼ Create a newsletter
- ▼ Create an invitation
- ▼ Create a contract
- ▼ Create a manuscript

Chapter 1
The Marriage Trifecta

...ther went on a Senior Citizen Trip to the racetrack in Cincinnati, met this old
...w to figure the odds, and set up the Marriage Trifecta, a sort of raffle in
...ends tried to guess the month, year, and groom of my wedding. Like a
...odds and pay-off for any number of combinations of husbands and
...ate the chart as I acquired and discarded new prospects. Practically
... in the Marriage Trifecta.
... same--in a pattern. Tilly raised her two girls, Mom and Aunt Kay
...sed her two girls my sister Lynne and me in the same way. Lynne,
...e same. There's a method to our madness.
... to cry, my mom would send me to my room. I'd storm up
...head in the stairwell and scream, "Cry harder . I can't hear
..."I still can't hear you. You must not really be crying. Cry
...ope, I still can't hear you," she'd say...

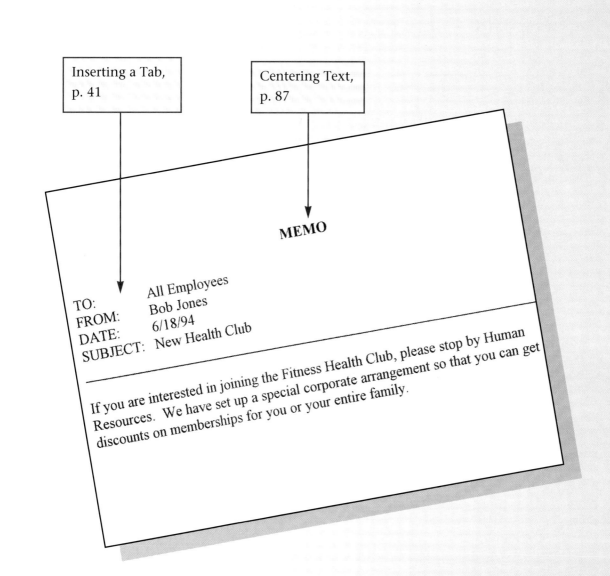

Inserting a Tab,
p. 41

Centering Text,
p. 87

MEMO

TO: All Employees
FROM: Bob Jones
DATE: 6/18/94
SUBJECT: New Health Club

If you are interested in joining the Fitness Health Club, please stop by Human Resources. We have set up a special corporate arrangement so that you can get discounts on memberships for you or your entire family.

Create a memo

1 Change the font to Times New Roman 14 point. This task covers font changes:

2 Type, center, and boldface the heading. See this task for help on this step:

3 Type **TO:**, press **Tab** twice, and type **All Employees**. Do this for each line of the memo "address." Rather than type the date, you can insert it automatically. See these tasks:

4 Draw a horizontal line. See this task:

5 Type the memo contents.

6 Save and print the memo. See these tasks on saving and printing:

7 Close the memo. See this task on closing a document:

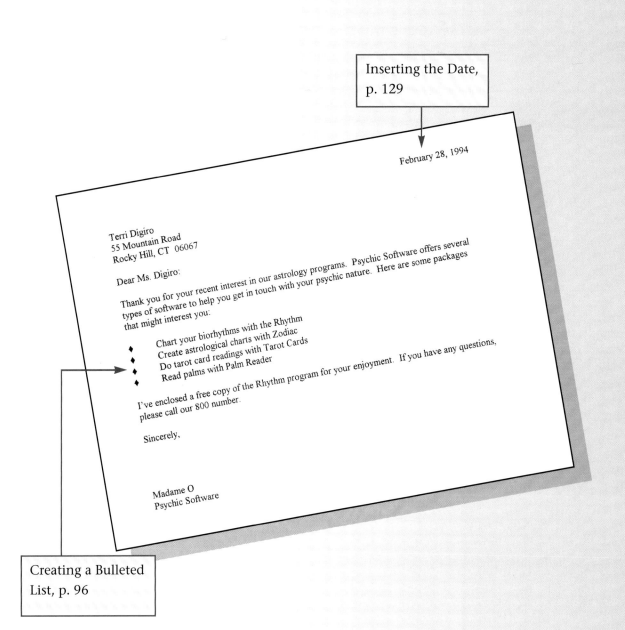

Inserting the Date,
p. 129

February 28, 1994

Terri Digiro
55 Mountain Road
Rocky Hill, CT 06067

Dear Ms. Digiro:

Thank you for your recent interest in our astrology programs. Psychic Software offers several types of software to help you get in touch with your psychic nature. Here are some packages that might interest you:

- Chart your biorhythms with the Rhythm
- Create astrological charts with Zodiac
- Do tarot card readings with Tarot Cards
- Read palms with Palm Reader

I've enclosed a free copy of the Rhythm program for your enjoyment. If you have any questions, please call our 800 number.

Sincerely,

Madame O
Psychic Software

Creating a Bulleted
List, p. 96

Create a business letter

1 Insert and right-align the date. These tasks explain how to complete this step:

2 Type the letter. The font used in this letter is Times New Roman 12 point. You may need to change the font. Create the bulleted list in the letter. See these tasks:

3 Save and print the letter. See these tasks on saving and printing:

4 Close the letter. See this task on closing a document:

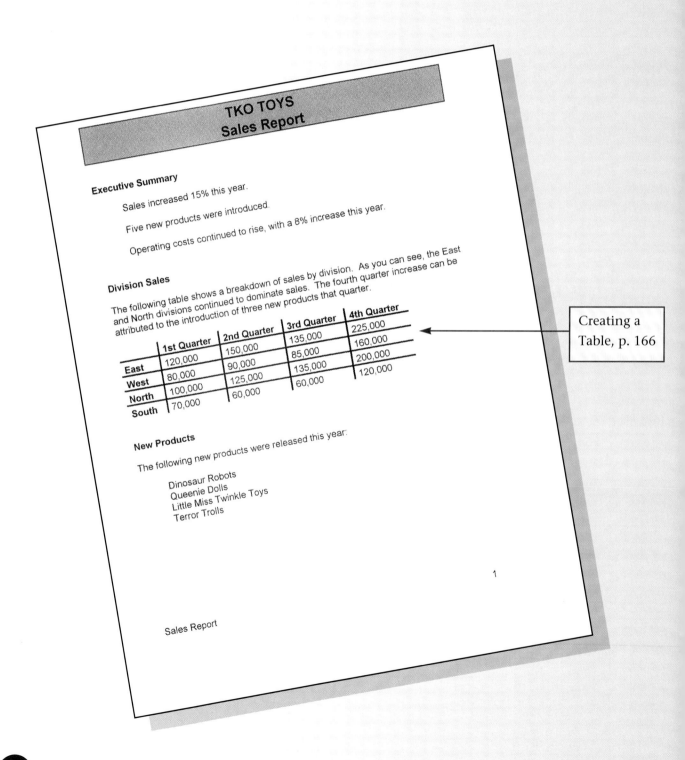

TKO TOYS
Sales Report

Executive Summary

Sales increased 15% this year.

Five new products were introduced.

Operating costs continued to rise, with a 8% increase this year.

Division Sales

The following table shows a breakdown of sales by division. As you can see, the East and North divisions continued to dominate sales. The fourth quarter increase can be attributed to the introduction of three new products that quarter.

	1st Quarter	2nd Quarter	3rd Quarter	4th Quarter
East	120,000	150,000	135,000	225,000
West	80,000	90,000	85,000	160,000
North	100,000	125,000	135,000	200,000
South	70,000	60,000	60,000	120,000

Creating a Table, p. 166

New Products

The following new products were released this year:

Dinosaur Robots
Queenie Dolls
Little Miss Twinkle Toys
Terror Trolls

1

Sales Report

Create a report

1 Type the report name. Then center it, make it bold, add a paragraph border, and a paragraph shade. The font used is Arial 18 point. These tasks cover how to apply the formatting changes:

2 Type the report text. The text is Arial 12-point type. The headings are bold. Don't forget the table! Here are the tasks to help with this step:

3 Add a footer with the report name and page number. The page number is right-aligned. See these tasks:

4 Save and print the report. See these tasks on saving and printing:

5 Close the report. See this task on closing a document:

Part X: Sample Documents

Making Text Bold, Italic, or Underlined, p. 80

Drawing a Horizontal Line, p. 158

Carole Simpson
150 Grapevine Road
Beverly Farms, MA 01916
508-921-3447

EDUCATION

Master of Business Administration, Boston University, Boston, Massachusetts.

Bachelor of Science degree in communications, Boston University, Boston, Massachusetts. Graduated magna cum laude.

EXPERIENCE

Vice President of Marketing, MRO Corporation.

- Manage staff of 30 public relations specialists, copy writers, and product designers.
- Coordinate and plan all marketing pieces: catalogs, promotional pieces, direct mail.
- Responsible for look and design of all company products.
- Responsible for budget of 1.2 million.

Director of New Products, MRO Corporation.

- Design and suggest new product lines.
- Work with product designers and engineers to ensure quality product.
- Coordinate product testing and product launches.
- Developed and launched 3 new product lines during tenure.
- New product lines generated 3.5 million in net revenue.

Advertising Director, S&O Advertising.

- Managed 15 account representatives, ensuring all clients received quality work.
- Directly worked for the top 2 accounts, designing and coordinating advertising campaigns.
- Solicited new clients.
- Added 7 new clients.

REFERENCES

Available upon request.

Create a resume

1 Type the name. The name, in this example, uses Arial 14-point type. It is centered and bold. See these tasks:

2 Type the resume. Change the font to 12-point type. Make the headings bold, draw the horizontal lines, italicize the job title, and create the bulleted items, as described in these tasks:

3 Save and print the resume. See these tasks on saving and printing:

4 Close the resume. See this task on closing a document:

Part X: Sample Documents

Changing the Font, p. 83

Broad Ripple News   SPRING 1994

VOLUME II

Butterfly Collection

Famed butterfly collector Jerome Hanley will be in Broad Ripple this weekend to display his collection of over 250 butterflies. Mr. Hanley has been to every continent, 50 different countries in his quest for the ultimate butterfly collection.

The collection will be on display in Hanley's Art Gallery from 10AM to 5PM all next week.

New Store Opens

Welcome to Broad Ripple Village the new shop Polka Dots. This new children's clothing store is open 10AM to 6PM., Monday through Saturday and features some of the finest children's fashions.

Kelley Sullivan, owner, says she's been to New York, California, and

Atlanta to select the best clothes for kids. The store will include infant clothes up to preteens. "If you have trouble finding unique, reasonably priced clothes for your kids, come to Polka Dots".

As a grand opening special, all merchandise will be 20% off for the month of March.

Annual Spring Fair

The Broad Ripple Spring Fair is scheduled for April 4 at the Broad Ripple Park. Art booths, food, and entertainment all make the fair the place to be.

This year over 50 local artists will be displaying their work. Some artists will be providing demonstrations and discussing artistic techniques.

Entertainment will be provided by the Spinsations, a local band. Also, clowns, jugglers, and storytellers will be around to delight the children attending.

Cost of admission is $14; children under 12 are free. For more information on the Fair, call Susan Corazato at 555-9011.

Inside...
Welcome new BRVA President
Renovation Plans for Park
Valuable Coupons

Adding a Paragraph Border, p. 138

Creating a Two-Column Document, p. 177

Create a newsletter

1 Type the newsletter banner. The first line is centered, bold, and uses Braggadocio 14-point type. The second line uses the same font in 12 point. See these tasks for help:

2 Draw a horizontal line. See this task:

3 Turn on two columns. See this task for help:

4 Format the headings. The headings are Arial 12-point type, and they are boldface. The article text is Arial 12-point type. See these tasks:

5 Shade the last section. See these tasks for help:

6 Insert and place the graphic. See these tasks for help:

7 Create a footer and insert a horizontal line in the footer. See thise task:

8 Save and print the newsletter. See these tasks on saving and printing:

Inserting a Graphic, p. 160

Create an invitation

1 Insert a graphic. This graphic uses clip art. The paragraph is centered. See this task:

Inserting a Graphic   *p. 160*

2 Type and center the heading. Indent the other lines with tabs. This text uses Brush Script MT 18-point type. See these tasks:

Changing the Font   *p. 83*

Changing the Font Size   *p. 85*

Centering Text   *p. 87*

3 Save and print the invitation. See these tasks on saving and printing:

Saving a Document   *p. 68*

Printing Your Document   *p. 193*

4 Close the invitation. See this task on closing a document:

Closing a Document   *p. 70*

Part X: Sample Documents

Indenting Text, p. 91

Fee and Representation Agreement

Attorney K. McShane and his client, _____, contract and agree to the following terms and conditions of representation:

The client, _____, hereby authorizes Attorney K. McShane to represent him without limitation in a claim for personal injury against all relevant parties.

The attorney for this action will be one-third of the gross recoveries (meaning recovery before deduction of medical or other expenses), but this percentage will increase to forty percent of the gross recovery if a lawsuit becomes necessary and is expressly authorized by the client.

The client will be responsible for payment of all expenses, including all expenses of investigation, litigation, and any other expenses necessary to this action.

The attorney agrees to represent her clients as zealously as possible within the bounds of law but states at the outset of this representation that no promises or guarantees as to specific outcome have been or can be made.

_____
Attorney

_____
Client

_____
Date

_____
Date

Create a contract

1 Type the heading. Make it italic and centered. This example uses Times New Roman 14-point type. See these tasks:

2 Type the contract. Indent the paragraphs. See this task:

3 Use the underscore to create the blank lines.

4 Save and print the contract. See these tasks on saving and printing:

5 Close the contract. See this task on closing a document:

Part X: Sample Documents

Double-Spacing a Document, p. 106

Chapter 1

The Marriage Trifecta

My grandmother went on a Senior Citizen Trip to the racetrack in Cincinnati, met this old guy who taught her how to figure the odds, and set up the Marriage Trifecta, a sort of raffle in which my family and friends tried to guess the month, year, and groom of my wedding. Like a bookie, she'd figure the odds and pay-off for any number of combinations of husbands and wedding dates. She'd update the chart as I acquired and discarded new prospects. Practically everyone I knew had a stake in the Marriage Trifecta.

We were all raised the same--in a pattern. Tilly raised her two girls, Mom and Aunt Kay the same, and Mom in turn raised her two girls my sister Lynne and me in the same way. Lynne, in turn, will raise her two girls the same. There's a method to our madness.

When I was little and used to cry, my mom would send me to my room. I'd storm up there just wailing. She'd stick her head in the stairwell and scream, "Cry harder . I can't hear you." I'd cry harder. She'd scream "I still can't hear you. You must not really be crying. Cry harder." I'd scream my head off. "Nope, I still can't hear you," she'd say. Finally I'd wear myself out. Tilly did the same thing to her.

1

Adding Page Numbers, p. 146

Create a manuscript

1 Type the title. This title uses Times New Roman 18-point type. The title is also bold and centered. See these tasks:

2 Type the manuscript. This document uses Times New Roman 12-point type. The document is also double-spaced, and the first line of each paragraph is indented. See these tasks for help on making these formatting changes:

3 Add page numbers, as described in this task:

4 Save and print the manuscript. See these tasks on saving and printing:

5 Close the manuscript. See this task on closing a document:

Glossary

block   Text that you select while in Block mode. A block can be a character, a word, a sentence, a paragraph, or any amount of text. After you select a block, you can perform different actions—copy it, delete it, enhance it, and so on.

button   A graphic displayed in the Power Bar or Button Bar that provides quick access to frequently used commands.

Button Bar   An on-screen area that displays buttons you can use to access frequently used commands.

carriage return   The method you use to end a line and start a new line. In WordPerfect, you can have two types of carriage returns: soft returns and hard returns. A soft return is inserted automatically by WordPerfect when you reach the end of a line. A hard return is inserted when you press Enter. Hard returns end a line and move the cursor to the start of the next line.

centering   An alignment option that centers text between the left and right margins.

Clipboard   A temporary storage place for text and graphics. When you cut or copy text or graphics, the item is stored in the Clipboard. The Clipboard is a Windows feature.

copy   An operation that duplicates a block of text. Text appears in both the original location and the location to which the text is copied.

data file   One of two essential parts of a merge operation. The data file stores the information that you want to insert into the main document (the form file). Each piece of information is stored in a field; a set of information is called a record.

default settings   Standard WordPerfect settings that are in effect each time you start the program.

dialog box   An on-screen window that appears when certain commands are selected. The dialog box prompts for additional information.

directory   A disk area that stores information about files. A directory is like a folder in a file cabinet. Within that folder, you can store several files.

document window   The area on-screen where you type text. You can have more than one document window open at a time.

DOS   An acronym for *disk operating system*. DOS manages the details of your system, such as storing and retrieving programs and files.

field   The variable information you enter in a merge letter. You create fields in a data file.

file   The various individual documents, such as reports, memos, and letters, that you store on your hard drive or floppy disk for future use.

font   The style, size, and typeface of a set of characters.

footer   Text that appears at the bottom of a printed document. Footers can appear on all pages, on even pages only, or on odd pages only.

form file   One of two essential parts of a merge operation. The form file contains the unchanging text of the document, as well as the merge codes that tell WordPerfect where to insert the variable information.

hard page break   A page break that you insert to force a break at a certain spot. A hard page break appears on-screen as a double-dashed line.

hard return   A type of return that is inserted when you press Enter. A hard return ends the line and moves the cursor to the start of the next line.

header   Text that appears at the top of a printed document. Headers can appear on all pages, on even pages only, or on odd pages only.

Help   An on-screen WordPerfect feature that displays a description of different topics and features.

insertion point   A tiny vertical bar that blinks. The insertion point marks the place, on-screen, where you begin typing text, deleting text, selecting a block, and so on.

left-justification   An alignment option that makes text line up along the left margin.

margins   The white space left around the four edges of the paper (left, right, top, and bottom).

menu   An on-screen list of WordPerfect options. You can select a menu option by pressing the letter that is highlighted in the menu option, such as the *S* in **S**ave.

merge code   A code that inserts a field or performs other action in a merge file.

mouse   An input device that enables you to move the cursor on-screen, select menu commands, and perform other operations.

Glossary

move   An operation that transfers a block of text from one location to another. The text appears only in the new location.

path   The route, through directories, to a program or document file. For example, the path C:\WPWIN60\WPDOCS\REPORT.WPD includes four elements. These elements are the disk drive (C:); the first directory (WPWIN60); the subdirectory, which is a directory within the first directory (WPDOCS); and the file name (REPORT.WPD).

Power Bar   An on-screen area that displays buttons you can use to access frequently used commands.

print buffer   The place in the printer's memory that stores text. When you print a document, text is sent from the computer to the printer. The printer stores the text in a print buffer until it is printed.

record   The collection of fields in a data file. A record stores one set of information about a person, for instance.

Reveal Codes   Hidden codes that WordPerfect inserts into your document. These codes can indicate tab spaces, carriage returns, margin settings, font changes, line spacing, and so on. Some codes contain information for headers and footers; these codes are usually singular. Other codes come in pairs where the first code turns on a feature and the second code turns off a feature.

right-justification   An alignment option that makes text line up along the right margin.

scroll bars   The bars at the bottom and right of the document window. You can use the bars to scroll through the document.

search string   A set of characters, such as a word or phrase, for which WordPerfect looks in search-and-replace operations.

soft page break   A page break that WordPerfect inserts automatically when you have entered enough text to fill a page. A soft page break appears on-screen as a dashed line.

soft return   A return that WordPerfect inserts automatically when you reach the end of the line. Soft returns are readjusted if you add or delete text.

status bar   The bottom line of the WordPerfect window. The status bar displays the current font choice as well as the location of the insertion point.

Thesaurus   A WordPerfect feature that enables you to look up, on-screen, synonyms and antonyms for a selected word. Synonyms are words with similar meanings. Antonyms are words with opposite meanings.

title bar   The bar that appears at the top of the window and displays the name of the program and, in some cases, the document name.

word wrap   A WordPerfect feature that eliminates the need to press Enter each time you reach the right margin. Instead, WordPerfect moves, or "wraps," text to the next line automatically.

Index

A

addressing envelopes, 197-198
aligning text, 87-95
appending
    rows to tables, 172-174
    text to documents, 28-31
attributes (text), 80-82

B

Backspace key, 51
blank lines, 37-38
blocks (text), 240
bold text, 80-82
borders, 136
bulleted lists, 96-98
business letters, 226-227
Button Bars, 17-18, 240
buttons, 240

C

carriage returns, 240
cascading menus, 10
cascading windows, 67
centering text, 87-88, 240
Clipboard, 56, 240
closing
    documents, 70-71
    menus, 16
codes
    merge codes, 241
    revealing, 38, 108-109, 242
columns (documents), 177-180
combining
    pages, 45
    paragraphs, 39-40
commands
    ... (ellipsis) following, 10
    selecting, 14-16
    see also individual menu
        listings
contracts, 236-237
copying text, 55-57, 240
cutting text, 58-60

D

data entry
    records (merge operations),
        207-209
    tables, 169-171
data files (merge operations),
    202, 240
    creating, 204-206
    records, 242
    saving, 210-211
date/time insertion, 129-130
default settings, 240
Delete key, 51
deleting, 168
    records, 209
    rows from tables, 175-176
    tabs, 43
    text, 51, 52
deselecting text, 50
dialog boxes, 10, 240
    Bullets and Numbers, 98, 101
    Create Data File, 205-206
    Create Form File, 213
    Delete Columns/Row, 176
    Envelope, 198
    Find and Replace Text,
        118-120
    Find Text, 115-116
    GoTo, 47
    Grammatik, 127-128
    Headers/Footers, 150, 153
    Image, 161-162
    Insert Columns/Row, 173-174
    Insert Field Name or Number,
        215-217
    Margins, 145
    Merge, 205, 221
    Open File, 73
    Page Numbering, 147-148
    Paragraph Border, 139-143
    Perform Merge, 221
    Print, 194-196
    Quick Data Entry, 206
    Save As, 69
    Select Printer, 192
    Speller, 122-123
    Tab Set, 104-105
    Thesaurus, 125
    Undelete, 54
    WordPerfect Characters,
        132-133
    Zoom, 187-188
directories, 240
displaying
    Button Bar, 17-18
    codes, 108-109
    Ruler Bar, 21-22
document windows, 240
documents
    checking grammar, 126-128
    closing, 70-71
    creating, 74-75
    displaying codes, 108-109
    editing, 111-113
    formatting, 78-79, 135-137
    graphics, 160-165
    navigating, 28, 34-36
    opening, 72-73
    Page Layout view, 186-188
    printing, 191-194
    sample documents, 223-239
    saving, 68-69
    spell checking, 121-123
    Typeover mode, 32-33
DOS (disk operating system), 241
double-spacing documents, 106-107
drag and drop editing, 56
drawing lines, 158-159

E

Edit menu commands
    Copy, 57
    Cut, 60
    Find, 115
    GoTo, 46-47
    Paste, 57, 60
    Replace, 118
    Undelete, 52-54
    Undo, 62
editing
    documents, 111-113
    headers/footers, 152-153
envelopes, 197-198
exiting WordPerfect for Windows,
    12-13

Index